ARGH!

TIM QUINN

WHAT THE GENERAL PUBLIC HAVE TO SAY ABOUT TIM QUINN

Stan Lee: 'Titanic Tim!'

Gyles Brandreth: 'Genius!'

Brian May: 'Tim Quinn is good for vibes!'

D Howett (no relation): 'A right rollicking read from the man who brought you *Hulk the Menace*, *Jet Lagg* and *The Fairly Amazing Spider-Hound*.'

CW00498570

publishing

ISBN 978-1-908630-44-5

Biography

£15.99 RRP

Cover design **Andrew Orton**

Also available:

with Dicky Howett
It's Even Bigger on the Inside

by Dicky Howett
Drawing Breath

ARGH!

TIM QUINN

Argh!

Second paperback edition published September 2016 by
Miwk Publishing Ltd, 45A Bell St, Reigate, RH2 7AQ.

ISBN 978-1-908630-44-5

A CIP catalogue record for this book is available from the British Library.

Design by Andrew Orton.
Typeset in Myriad Pro and Minion Pro.
© Eric Fish (photographs on pages 133 and 140).

Printed and bound by TJ International, Cornwall.

www.miwkpublishing.com
This product was lovingly Miwk made.

To Jane – my life.

CHAPTER 1

ARGH!

'ARGH!' My mother always swore that was my very first word on planet Earth. Hardly a wonder when you consider what my first sight must have been. I was born on Monday the 21st of September 1953 at 6:00am in Park House nursing home in Liverpool. The mini hospital was run and staffed by nuns. That's nuns of the period, not today's bright and trendy looking nuns. So my very first sight on planet Earth was of a period nun in the full black habit, cosh-rosary, and cowl, complete with surgical face-mask. 'ARGH!' indeed.

For this was Liverpool at the midpoint of the Twentieth Century. Priests, nuns and, worst of all, Irish Christian Brothers roamed the streets freely with a religious system straight out of the Middle Ages. 'Thou shalt not...' was the Golden Rule. Is it any wonder I took to reading *The Beano* at the earliest opportunity? Liverpool in the mid-Fifties was a city designed by Victorian architects and Adolf Hitler. Hermann Goering to be precise. His Luftwaffe had cut a swathe through the place, and ten years on from the blitz, overgrown bombsites had become part of the landscape. Together with the abandoned army camp, Fort Crosby, on the banks of the River Mersey, Liverpool was the perfect playground for this kid to grow up in. And things were abuzz. I was born in perfect time for Rock & Roll and the plethora of naughty kids that exploded from Scottish weekly comic books during the Fifties. Menaces, Perils, Smashers, Minxes, Dodgers and Bash Street Kids led the revolution against authority of all kinds. Peashooters and bricks aimed at the back of a teacher's head made us see exactly how ridiculous the pomposity of the established order really was. Satire started in the comics, years before David Frost and company picked up on it.

Oddly, the first two years of my life are a complete blank. Something so bloody awful must have been happening to me on a daily basis that I have removed all memories from my brain simply to stay sane(ish). I see from history books that Everest was conquered and Queen Elizabeth II was crowned, giving birth to television aerials popping up on rooftops across the land during this amnesiac time.

One thing I do know is that I was named after a comic book character. Yes, my Mum had loved Tiger Tim and the Bruin Boys in the *Rainbow* comic when she was growing up in the Twenties, and so when it came to name her favourite child there was only one name to choose. I guess that kind of set things in motion for my future. Speaking of which, my very earliest memory is of my Mum handing me a stick of charcoal and telling me to go and draw on my bedroom wall. I was two years and eleven months of age and we had just that day moved into our first home, a huge rambling Victorian house twenty minutes from the centre of Liverpool. As luck would have it, I drew a hardboiled egg, which with a bit of added scribble and a smiley face passed as a recognizable hedgehog. I had a character that I could start telling stories about. And start telling stories I did. It was a big bedroom with huge walls. As befits the 1950s, the first story I told in five pictures had the hedgehog (who I named Tim... I didn't know many names at that age) finding a space rocket in his back garden. Luckily, it was the 1950s because space rockets were easy to draw then, being simple cigar-shapes with fins and portholes rather than the complicated monstrosities post *Star Wars*. I remember that I added a letter slot in the front door of the rocket so the inhabitants could receive their daily mail. Tim climbed aboard, traveled across space and landed on the moon where he found he could leap tall distances in a single bound. That was it. If there are any movie producers reading this, the rights are still available. Hey, I was only two and a bit!

Learning to read

I hate school! Third from right, front row.

Schooldays – what can I say? I found the majority of teachers daft although I am eternally grateful to Sisters Monica and Ethelreda at the Ursuline Convent for helping me crack the code of Riting and Reading. And one wonderful form teacher I had for two years at The Mount. Mr Fitzgerald turned his whole class into readers by introducing us to Conan Doyle's *The Lost World*. Still a favourite book, and I can still hear Mr Fitzgerald's accent reading Sir John Roxton's part. The rest of the teachers left something to be desired. The only thing they inspired me to do was play truant and look forward to turning sixteen so I could get the hell out of Limbo. For this was a Catholic school where we were encouraged to look ahead at all times to Death, when we would move over to one of three places: Limbo, Purgatory or Hell. I was age six when they dropped that one on me, and seven when I decided they were all nutters. It was after my first (and last) confession. I didn't have a clue what to put up as my sin of the day so when the priest asked me to confess my sins I replied: 'I didn't take my medicine today.' I was on a course of Minadex to promote growth in seven year-olds. The priest didn't skip a beat: 'Say two Hail Marys and an Our Father and I absolve you of the sin of not taking your medicine.' Kind of like the 'Get Out of Jail Free Card' in Monopoly. And that was it with me and religion. And school.

I found I had a knack for looking out of the classroom window and imagining all sorts of stories as I wandered freely with my dog Rags around Liverpool. There were two other boys in my class with the same talent. At age 10 we teamed-up to produce a weekly comic to sell to our classmates. I came up with the title, *The Banger*, and the main character, Wat Why, a dog. This was in 1963, a time way before photocopiers, so turning out copies of our work was a pain in the neck after the initial enthusiasm for the project wore off. We did three issues in all with twelve pages in each edition. I remember that the very final page showed we had already moved on. It was eight empty panels laid out in typical comic book format with the title: YOUR CHANCE TO MAKE YOUR OWN COMIC STRIP!

Wat Why and The Banger. School comic.

Comics were a huge part of my life by this time. What a great period to grow up in. Every week the newsagent's shelf groaned and sagged under the sheer weight of the comic weeklies. Such a variety of stories exploded from the pages of titles like *Lion*, *Valiant*, *TV Express*, *Buster*, and *The New Hotspur*. On one page you would have an adventure set on Mars followed by stories in the Wild West, under the ocean, in deepest jungle, highest mountain, prehistory, and public school. Robots, spacemen, cowboys, pirates, schoolboys, detectives, and explorers became my pals. Over in the funnies, *Oor Wullie* and *The Broons* bi-annual books became my favourites. Written in the thickest Scottish dialect, which I still drop into on occasion, these glorious books captured exactly what it was like to be a boy in the Twentieth Century.

And then there were the American comic books. What a joy to find the odd newsagent who had the imports displayed on a whizzy comic book rack featuring the best from so many US publishers. Dell, DC, Harvey, Archie, Gold Key, Atlas, and then… Marvel Pop Art Productions! And how lucky was I? We had let the top floor of our house to an American family. The Dad was over here working for the US Air Force out of Burtonwood base in Liverpool. He would take brother Mike and I onto the base to see the planes and, even better, have a rummage through the PX where they sold American comics and candy. Tootsie Rolls and Dime bars, no less, but all the very latest comics hot off the press. Ohh… the excitement!

I wouldn't describe myself as a violent boy although the list of weapons in my armory might make you think otherwise. Colt pistols and holster with silver Lone Ranger bullets, a luger, Captain Cutlass's very own cap pistol, a machine gun with realistic sound, various spud guns, peashooter, catapult, Buffalo Bill rifle, Dan Dare's ray gun, and a bloody great sheaf knife strapped to my thigh over my shorts and school blazer and cap. On top of this I had legions of toy soldiers that I would slaughter daily in battles across my bedroom floor. This was an army like no other with US Civil War soldiers fighting alongside WW1 and WW2 Nazis, Tommies, Japanese kamakazi pilots and Robin Hood and his Merry Men. A real war to end all wars.

My grandfather on Mum's side had already coloured my view of war long before John Lennon suggested giving peace a chance. Pop, as we called him, had got off to a bad start in life by being born just at the right time to have to fight in two world wars. He never forgave the political bastards who sent his generation into Hell. Fooled by the jingoistic media of the day, he joined the Royal Flying Corps by lying about his age when he was just fifteen. He soon fell out with his so-called superior officer who referred to him as a 'little shit'. Not a smart thing to do with Pop. One grim day he snapped and broke the officer's nose. 'I can still hear the crack,' he would beam whenever recounting the tale during my childhood. Amazingly he wasn't shot but rather court-martialed and sent into the military in the trenches, where his British made gas mask proved faulty and he inhaled a near lethal dose of mustard gas which sent him back to Blighty, days before his troop were shot to bits. During the early sixties when it looked as though WW3 was on its way, he tried to calm any fears I might have by saying that he would shoot me in both feet rather than let me be called up. As I was only about eight or nine years of age at the time I had certain reservations about this. The top floor of Pop's house was a real armory containing all sorts he had picked up during the two wars. Machine guns, rifles, pistols, bullets by the ton, grenades, bayonets, a bazooka, and even a Samurai sword! Brother Mike and I loved getting togged up with all this real weaponry and battling it out round the house. I remember seeing a grenade come bouncing down the staircase towards me during one major skirmish. Tis a wonder we are both still here.

We got our telly in 1960, in perfect timing for Gerry Anderson's Tex Tucker in *Four Feather Falls*. As puppet shows go, it was a mighty leap from the wetter-than-wet *Torchy the Battery Boy*. I was hooked from episode one at the cast of highly likeable characters, a staple of Anderson's series. I was already a cowboy before *FFF*. I don't think there was a day of the week without a Western series on the TV. *Cheyenne, Bronco Laine, Tenderfoot, Laramie, Bonanza, The Lone Ranger, Hoppalong Cassidy, Rawhide, Wagon Train, The Rifleman…* the list was endless. Once home from school, off would come the cap and blazer to be replaced by Davy Crockett's coonskin hat or a full Sioux Chief feathered headdress as I would hunt for palefaces or outlaws out in the garden. This is how West Liverpool was won. There was one cowboy I couldn't stand though. He even had a full-page colour strip on the back of *TV Comic*. This was the original Milky Bar Kid. Speccy little git. Didn't like his chocolate bar and didn't like him. Oddly, more than fifty years on, the thought of him still gets my goat. Time to let it go. I thought he was a waste of space in *TV Comic* even though he had only replaced the equally dreadful weekly story about *The Ladybird Adventurers*, which was an advertisement for Woolworth's own kids' clothing line.

Yes, telly was good. There was an air of experimentation about it back then. Even though there were only two channels and programming from 5pm to midnight, they crammed a lot in. Westerns, detectives, plays, comedy, variety, pop, and some pretty wacky cartoons such as *Foo-Foo & Go-Go*, and *Rocky & Bulwinkle*. The Granada TV area was really cooking. Their local news shows, *People & Places*, and *Scene at 6:30*, were run by real journalists (remember them?) with a flair for presenting, news, and entertainment. They were fun shows to watch and gave me a pull to work in TV at some point in my life. What a difference today's dreary local news shows are. You could be anywhere in the country and they are all the same. Luckily I'm not one to moan.

And then there was music. Oh yes. I was growing up in Liverpool, you see, in the fifties and early sixties. Music was everywhere, especially in our house. Mum and Dad bought our 3D Radiogram in 1957. Its sound filled the house with my parents' varied choice in music. Beethoven, Mozart, Liszt, Strauss, Deanna Durbin, Glen Miller, Roaring Twenties Jazz Age hits, bloody John McCormack, Calypso, Harry Belafonte, and the Beverley Sisters. My very first record was the *Jack & Jill Party Record* from 1957. It was advertised in my *Jack & Jill* weekly and featured all the characters from the comic attending a party. It was one of those cardboard records that were big at the time. It is pinned to the office wall behind me as I type, signed by Rolf Harris (many years later when I was on his TV show) who did all the voices.

It was 1962 when I started buying my own records. First up was the *James Bond Theme* by the John Barry Seven followed by *Dance On* by The Shadows. Both instrumentals get me to this day. Talk about a groove going on. Great start to the collection that now fills a whole room of my house, but back then something dreadful happened. I bought my first LP. Cliff Richard & The Shadows in *The Young Ones*. Now keep in mind this was one hell of an expense for a boy on pocket money. Thirty-two shillings and sixpence. That's a lot of comic books. And it was bloody dreadful, crammed full of the ghastly kind of tunes that filled out a pop movie of the period. I swore I would never buy another LP. Thanks, Cliff. And then I heard *Please Please Me*. It stopped me in my tracks as I came into my house from an afternoon's playing in the snow and ice on one of the coldest winters since records began. It was Sunday 20th January 1963. I marked it in my Enid Blyton Diary. Everything changed for me that day. That was the moment the sixties truly began. I stood there in the kitchen transfixed by the radio. Nothing had ever sounded like that. They say nothing is black and white. That record was. I remember thinking that I was glad I was in my tat – torn jeans and baggy ripped sweater. I knew whoever was making this sound would be dressed like this. So it was quite a surprise a week or so later when I saw my first photograph of The Beatles. They were in suits! Even so, there was something so coolly tat about those faces and that hair. By then I'd bought the single and loved both A and B sides. So by the time they released their first LP a couple of months later I was ready to make that gamble. I'd been let down by Cliff but this was The Beatles, and guess what? They came from Liverpool. Even so, it was with a little trepidation that I dropped the stylus on Side one for the first play. That fear was instantly kicked out by the countdown to *I Saw Her Standing There*: 'One, Two, Three, Four...' Every track grabbed me in a different way, right through to the cheer of triumph at the end of Side Two's *Twist & Shout*. Cosmic, Gamma Powered music. The Beatles. I do believe they have come up in conversation every day since. Bigger on the Inside than Jesus? I should say so!

CHAPTER 2

1961–1965
Love – SHOUT IT!

AT AGE EIGHT I FELL IN LOVE FOR THE FIRST TIME WITH DUSTY SPRINGFIELD AFTER SEEING HER WITH HER BAND THE SPRINGFIELDS AT THE LIVERPOOL EMPIRE THEATRE. SHE WAS TWENTY-FOUR AT THE TIME AND THE AGE DIFFERENCE GOT IN THE WAY OF OUR ROMANCE. THAT AND THE FACT THAT SHE WAS A LESBIAN AND I WASN'T.

AT AGE ELEVEN AND A HALF I FELL IN LOVE FOR THE SECOND TIME WITH LADY PENELOPE IN THE PAGES OF *TV21* COMIC. I HAD NO PROBLEM WITH THE AGE DIFFERENCE OR THE FACT THAT SHE WAS A PUPPET, BUT IT WAS NOT TO BE.

CHAPTER 3

1963–1968

Beatles, Books & Telly

By August of 1963 The Beatles were exploding in every direction. I now had their first three singles and first LP together with a bedroom full of press cuttings. What could be better? I'll tell you what could be better. Mum coming into my room with tickets for brother Mike and I to see the boys live at the Odeon Cinema up the railway track in Southport. Yes, LIVE! Not on screen but LIVE! I love my mother! And what a day Monday 26th August 1963 turned out to be. Three great bands on the bill: The Fourmost, Gerry and the Pacemakers and The Beatles. Not bad for 8/6d! We got there early to hang around the Stage Door. No Fabs spotted but I did get Brian O'Hara of The Fourmost's autograph and a tack out of his Chelsea Boot. The show itself was … Fab, what else?! I have no words to describe it other than that the rhythm and beat of that show is still vibrating through my solar system. We had good seats up front and I do remember that George Harrison had really plastered on the make-up about a yard thick. Cool look! I also remember that when The Beatles took the stage the whole cinema erupted. I was yelling for Ringo until the girl in front of me turned round with a face of thunder and roared: 'SHURRUP!' Obviously a Pete Best fan.

Between comics and music and telly, books were a big part of my life from Year Dot. Mum had been a librarian until Hitler had bombed her library. That was the way she told it so I always pictured the man himself at the controls of the Fuhrer Bomber, looking down on Merseyside and saying: 'There! That's the library we must destroy. Bombs away!' Despite that old bastard, Mum brought books into my life from an early age and I have always loved the feel, smell, sight, and very paper of books. It was a Big Deal day when Mum took me to get my first Library Card. Still got it, of course. The very first book I read from cover to cover was *Noddy and the Magic Rubber*, which gives some qualms to my American friends, particularly when I then tell them that I won a *Blue Peter* badge in 1964. The badge was for sending in a 'very interesting idea for our programme'. I have no idea what that idea was but I am delighted that it was very interesting. *Blue Peter* was the BBC's finest children's magazine programme, dropping seeds of interest in a million subjects into kids' heads for over fifty years. Noddy was the creation of Enid Blyton, the finest writer for children ever! I went on to read shelf-loads of her books through my childhood. I've yet to come down from the *Magic Faraway Tree*.

As well as TV Westerns, I also loved the various detective series of the sixties. *The Avengers* (non-Mighty), *77 Sunset Strip*, *Danger Man*, but especially *The Prisoner*. This show was so in tune with the times, and even had The Beatles' *All You Need is Love* playing in the final episode. During the school summer holidays in '68, I got a call from my elder brother Mike. He had got himself a job in The Village, no less. Turns out The Prisoner's prison was not in some faraway exotic land but rather in North Wales at a place called Portmeirion. Mike told me to pack my bags and come on down as he had organized a summer job for me in the village itself! It is a truly breathtaking place. A real escape from planet Earth. The very air is different somehow to anywhere else. I was given a chalet, just like No. 6's, all meals and £7.00 a week for my services as a dogsbody. I did stuff. Dishes in the hotel kitchen, light bulbs in the chalets, litter out of the ponds. At 6pm every night, the general public were turfed out and the Village became mine. I bought a tinny record player and soon Donovan, the Lovin' Spoonful, and the Incredible String Band were adding to the atmosphere. No small thanks to my elder brother, a cloud of marijuana smoke hovered over Portmeirion that summer. He was keen to get me converted to the weed. We sat and watched a sunrise one morning. Mike lovingly rolling a joint, took a huge drag, closed his eyes and handed it to me. I looked at the sunrise over the Village and then back to him with his eyes closed missing everything. It was one of those turning points. He could keep his joint. I have to say that he has, and very happily too. He was last seen heading into the Back of Beyond in the outback of Australia where he joined a tribe of Aborigines. The funny thing is that back then everybody always made the mistake of thinking I was the stoned one. Mike had a straighter look. A look he has since lost. It was during this summer that I wrote my first (and last) poem. Inspired by the setting and Donovan, the opening line ran, 'The multi-coloured jester ran through the rain, his smile a disguise for 1,000 years of pain…' Exactly. Hey, don't blame me. It was the sixties and there was a dope cloud hovering.

The poet at Portmeirion in 1968.

Meanwhile, back at school, I encountered the Smarmy Teacher. I would enter the classroom and he would stop me in my tracks with the question:

ST: What are you, Quinn?
Me: I don't know. What am I, sir?
ST: You're a clown, Quinn, a clown. What are you?
Me: I'm a clown, sir. A clown.

Now fair enough, life must be pretty crappy for teachers like that and I suppose they must take their perks where they can, but even so. This wasn't a one-off occasion. It was every bloody lesson. Enough to give you a complex… if you didn't like clowns, that is. Unfortunately for ST, I did like clowns. Not the awful children's entertainer type who put on a red nose and thought they were immediately comic. No, not them but the real clowns. A tremendous moment in my life had been the day Coco the Clown visited my class back when I was a six year-old. He was promoting road safety and telling us how to look left, look right and look left again. Now Coco was a real clown with a rich history in the circus. Even more wonderful for me was that he was a character in my weekly *TV Comic* where he featured in a beautifully drawn strip. The moment he walked into my classroom was the moment that I realized for sure that comic book characters are real. So I have kind of always had a thing for real clowns. Calling me one didn't rate high on the punishment scale. The fact was though that I wasn't a clown in class. I was the semi-conscious guy at the back looking out the window. But, as things turned out, I probably have that teacher to thank for my life turning out as it has.

CHAPTER 4

1969

Circus Boy

I left school at the end of the sixties without a clue as to my future. The advice I'd been given by the school Careers Officer went like this:

CO: What are your interests?
Me: I like music, drawing and writing.
CO: Drawing, eh?
Me: Yeah, I particularly like comic book art.
CO: Hmm. What you should do is go to Lewis' department store and see if they need somebody to write out the price tags that go in the shop windows.

That was it. The extent of advice for a life in the Arts from my old school. Thank you. Very insightful. I walked out of the room thinking, what a git. Not that I had any other ideas in my head. However, the morning after I left school I was asked by my elder brother just what I hoped to do now. I told him that I just wanted to do something to prove I was alive. Not a bad plan really. After saying this, my old teacher's clown liturgy came to mind. On a whim, I packed a bag with undies and socks and a clean shirt and jeans, and took off for the coach station. I bought a one-way ticket up coast to Blackpool, where I walked from the station to the tower itself. Finding the Stage Door to the Blackpool Tower Circus, I knocked. And knocked again. After a pause it was opened by one of the most famous faces from the circus world. Charlie Cairoli had been a mainstay of BTC for nearly 40 years as head clown. And here he was in full make-up complete with bowler hat, looking me up and down. 'What do you want?' he asked. 'Any jobs going?' He looked me in the eye for a full minute of silence before opening the door further and nodding for me to enter. 'Follow me,' he said, leading the way to his dressing room. He sat me down in front of a mirror and proceeded to apply all sorts of slop to my face. A wig and jolly clothes were added. And so it was that 24 hours after leaving school I made my debut as a clown alongside Charlie and his troupe in the ring of the Blackpool Tower Circus to an audience of what seemed like thousands. My job was to throw buckets of water in the direction of Charlie but to make sure I missed with every one. I would then have paste and water thrown at me and I must make sure that each bucket hit me. It did. Those clowns were good. Another part of my job was to act as Ringboy (I hope they have changed that title by now), a virtual stagehand, carrying and rolling props in and out of the ring. As most of the props would have elephants or tigers standing on them they were a dead weight and you had to find a way to carry or spin them into the ring double-quick so as not to slow down the whole show which ran at breakneck speed. For the first few weeks I was also the guy with a bucket who had to race into the ring to clean up if the elephants left anything in their wake. They usually did. All teen self-consciousness left me forever after the first week of doing this.

Charlie was a funny guy. I don't think I ever saw him smile. He would always come and stand beside me during the flying trapeze act. Each performance he would say exactly the same thing: 'I only watch this in case one of them falls.' He would then tut in disappointment at the end of each act that the trapeze artist survived.

In an attempt to figure out who/what/why I was, I had decided to become a vegetarian on the coach ride up to Blackpool. Not as easy a task back then as it is today. There were no vegetarian meals to be found in stores so you had to figure it out yourself. As my job as clown/ringboy was pretty strenuous I had to figure it out swiftly as energy levels were all important. To begin with I would buy a chunk of cheese and a loaf of bread. Very filling but… The lot of the circus animals was a miserable one. To see elephants and tigers being paraded round the ring to the squawks and screeches of the audience was a depressing sight. Behind the scenes the animals were kept in cramped conditions, which made my vegetarian sense tingle.

'You're a clown, Quinn!' Blackpool Tower Circus. My first job.

I'd booked into a seedy boarding house. My room was in the attic and I felt very lonely whenever I returned there. No emails. No mobile. No Facebook. No instant communication with the outside world. Just me. The boarding house had a bathroom that gave me the creeps. There was something in the bath. To this day I don't know what it was and nor do I want to know, but it kept me out the bath the entire time I was there. That could well be the reason I caught fleas at one point. Possibly from the circus or possibly from the boarding house. Itchy. Between shows I'd go and sit on the pier with my loaf of bread and watch the seagulls go by. I looked a little curly-headed innocent and consequently attracted the passing trade in nonces. They would come and sit next to me and gradually work their way closer up the bench until our legs would touch in what I guess they must have seen as a courting gesture. When this failed to get the hoped for response from me, they would pull out a wallet and flash the ten shilling notes within. I was very polite the first few times this happened and simply made my excuses and left. After a month or so though I hit upon a brilliant way to get out of this situation whenever it arose. I would shout in a really loud voice the words 'fuck' and 'off'. It worked a dream and I have applied it on many occasions since with equal success even though my nonce attracting days are long over.

One thing became clear as the months went on. I wasn't much of a clown. Yes, I could throw buckets of water and slop like the best of them but the Chaplin/Coco instinct was nowhere to be found in my genes. And so at the end of the season when Charlie Cairoli asked about my plans I answered truthfully, 'Well I know I'm not a clown, despite what my teacher may have said.' Charlie nodded in agreement. 'This is true,' he said. He then told me about an old Music Hall in Leeds and suggested I might find work backstage there for the panto season. I had no better idea, so, my circus and flea-ridden days behind me, I hitched a ride over to Leeds.

CHAPTER 5

1969–1972

Good Old Days

Leeds was a fairly dour place to me back then. Keep in mind this is pre-Harvey Nicks days. It suited the phrase, it's grim up North. I found the theatre, The World Famous Leeds City Varieties Music Hall. There were two identical huge twins sitting in the box office, both with owl-like thick tin rim specs. They pointed my way to the Stage Door, down a tiny alleyway littered with dustbins and overflowing garbage. I walked through the door and found myself.

The City Varieties is definitely bigger on the inside. It was like stepping back in time to a world full of Dickensian characters. The theatre was over 200 years-old. It was mid-morning as I headed up a set of stairs, across the Green Room and up another three steps to the stage itself. The theatre was in darkness but I could hear somebody thirty-feet above me clambering around in the Fly gallery. He stuck his head over the rail and called down: 'Yeah?' I called up: 'Any jobs going? 'A trail of fag ash descended from on high. 'Wait!' he called. Minutes later he joined me on the stage, puffing and panting, fag still in mouth, ash all down his front, slicked back jet black hair, which I later found out to be coloured with boot polish. This was Wally, Stage Manager supreme. 'Do you know how to work the limes?' he asked. I didn't even know what the limes were. 'Be back here at two and I'll show you before the

Leeds City Varieties Music Hall

show begins at two-thirty.'

The limes were hardly brain surgery but still quite tricky to handle. Up in the gods was the Lime Box, a tiny booth for two spotlights operated by touching carbon rods and a boost of electricity. My fellow lime man was 'Old Pop' who looked as if he had been there since the theatre's opening night. The spotlights were of similar age. The show was *Snow White and the Seven Dwarfs*, which was advertised on the posters as WITH 7 REAL LIVE DWARFS! I guess this was as opposed to the dead variety other theatres featured. I found that Old Pop would sometimes doze off during the show. It tended to get very hot in the Lime Box and by the time you've seen the same show fifty times or more I could see his problem. There would be a splutter of carbon rods and his light would go out, literally.

For me it was a fun show and a most beautiful theatre. The same family, the Josephs, had run the place since before WW2. In my first week there while sweeping out the attic I discovered a poster advertising the Eight Lancashire Lads imminent arrival at the theatre. Charlie Chaplin had been one of the lads. The place really hadn't changed a bit since Victorian times. The BBC were there regularly to film a long running TV series, *The Good Old Days*, which was basically a night in a Victorian music hall, starring a variety of entertainers from Arthur Askey, Ken Dodd, Charlie Drake, Albert Modley, Ted Ray and Bruce Forsyth to Frankie Vaughan. Everybody, including the audience, would dress in Victorian costume so that, apart from the TV cameras, it was like stepping back through time. I remember Lonnie Donegan doing a double-take when he saw me and saying: 'I see you have come in disguise as Arlo Guthrie.' Arlo and I did share a similar look at the time.

The BBC would turn up late on a Saturday night with two huge outside broadcast vans that filled the alley at the back of the theatre. We stagehands would strip down whatever show was currently running and carry in all the props and gear for *The Good Old Days*, setting up backcloths for each act. We would get out round 4am and be back for first rehearsal by 10am. By this time the cameras would be in place. There were just three so as to not intrude too much on the Victorian atmosphere for the audience. One would be placed at the back of the stalls, another in a theatre box stage right, and the third at stalls right. I'm sure Dicky Howett would like to know the exact type of camera used so I will apply my technical knowledge here to say they were bloody great big ones. The dress rehearsal would take place at 6pm and the audience would be let in by 7:45pm for kick off at 9pm. As the series had already been running since the fifties, it was very rare for anything to go wrong during the recording. The only overruns I remember were when Ken Dodd topped the bill and that was par for the course. The audience would usually be out no later than 10:45pm while we stage crew did the reverse of the previous night, stripping *The Good Old Days* and resetting for Monday's show. All fun and all very exciting.

One incident comes to mind while filming *The Good Old Days*. I'm such an innocent, just seventeen, walking down the stairs from the Flys to the Green. On a window ledge at the bottom of the stairs sits Eartha Kitt dressed in Victorian green silk. She is looking up the staircase. She is looking up the staircase into my eyes. Directly into my eyes. Eartha Kitt is looking directly into my eyes. The Universe has come to a sudden stop because Eartha Kitt is looking directly into my eyes and she won't stop. There are twenty-four steps to climb down and her eyes don't blink or waver. I have to make you understand the full shuddering impact of that moment in my life. I was raised a Catholic in the fifties being sent to the nuns at age four followed by an eternity under the iron fist of the Irish Christian Brothers ('We will instil a fear of God in your child'.). There had been only boys at my school. No girls. And certainly no Eartha Kitt.

When I tell people my Eartha Kitt story, I always pause at this point so that they can say: 'Go on. What happened next?' I then take up the story. Her eyes followed me all the way to the kettle across the Green Room. When I turned from pouring myself a cup, she was still staring directly into my eyes. Pause. 'And then what?' Nothing. She was called on stage for her and I retreated back to the Flys.

'Not much of a story,' say my listeners. Maybe not to them and maybe not to you but to me, as I type these words, I am transported effortlessly back forty-five years to share a passionate moment in Time with the one and only Eartha Kitt. And I know for a fact that despite what she sang and how she was dressed on that occasion, she was no old-fashioned girl. Eartha Kitt, Catwoman, looked directly into my eyes and stayed there for the rest of my life. That, Simon Cowell, is

Star Quality.

Another memorable sex bomb who trod the boards at the Varieties was Barbara Windsor. I'd enjoyed her performances in everything from *The Rag Trade* onwards but nothing for me beats the award winning moment she walked out of her dressing room towards the toilet at the end of the corridor. Passing me she smiled the famous grin and said the immortal line: ' 'Ello, darlin'!' That would have been more than enough to make my day. The fact that she was stark naked made my decade. Yes, I was enjoying the theatrical life.

In my second month at the theatre I started writing for comics. Not comic books but comics as in comedians. Jimmy Cricket and Little & Large appeared in an edition of *The Good Old Days* and mentioned they were looking for scriptwriters. Standing in the wings, listening to their material, I thought it would be impossible to write anything much worse, and so I picked up a pen. I knocked up two scripts each, learned to type, and mailed them off to their agents. Amazingly all four scripts were accepted and I got a cheque for £25.00 each by return mail! That was a lot of comic books and records back then! Bingo! I suddenly realized I could write stuff. School certainly hadn't helped me come to this belief. If anything it had done the opposite. But school was now months ago. I was waking up…

By this time, one of my current favourite TV series was *Monty Python's Flying Circus*. I was over the moon when I heard they were going to do a theatre tour for the first time and pitch up in Leeds at the Grand Theatre. Turned out it was a night off for the City Varieties so I made sure I was working backstage at the Grand that day. Before the show, I carried a cup of tea into John Cleese's dressing room. We started chatting about the City Varieties, which is a theatre he wanted to see. I raved on about my time there and just how special the place was. I suddenly realized that sitting to one side of the dressing room was Eric Idle, dressed only in an old raincoat and flat cap. He didn't say a word but stared intently at me. John questioned me more about the history of the Varieties and I filled him in but I suddenly started stammering as the intensity of Idle's inspection grew ever more invasive. I turned and looked at him. He carried on staring. No smile, just the stare. Very odd. Very off-putting. And nothing like Eartha! Good show though.

I'm many pages into my life story and I can't believe I haven't mentioned how great I am yet. Yes, there's a reason Bob Dylan wrote the song Mighty Quinn. Spike Milligan, All Time King of Comedy, is the reason. In my head. Spike came to the theatre with his one-man show. During the afternoon, he wandered over to where I was sat backstage, drawing a cartoon strip. He looked at one of the pictures and started laughing. Yes, Spike Milligan was laughing at my cartoon! I'll repeat that. SPIKE MILLIGAN WAS LAUGHING AT MY CARTOON! And it got better. He then said these very words: 'That's funnier than anything I have ever written.' Now let me be the first to say that it most certainly wasn't. BUT, I made Spike Milligan laugh! I'm cool, I am. So push off anyone who disagrees. The cartoon? It showed a dog super-hero, the Shocking Sockstick, wearing a tartan sock on his head and carrying a curved tree branch in one paw as he swung upside-down from a trapeze above Manhattan. The caption read: 'Meanwhile, on an old abandoned trapeze high over New York City...' Comedy Gold! I have been a complete arrogant bastard ever since that day. Thanks, Spike.

The City Varieties closed each summer from June through September. In my first season there I had joined NATKE, a union for backstage workers that promised to get you a job in a London theatre at any time. So during that first Summer break I called in at the NATKE office in London. They gave me an address of a venue in Soho that needed a stagehand. It turned out to be Raymond's Revue Bar, an 'exclusive' strip joint. Now that was a very strange experience for this Catholic schoolboy. The girls were fun and funny backstage with a certain to-hell-with-it attitude about life. Standing in the wings, it was a little stomach-turning to see the look on the faces of the audience as the girls went about their work. Paul Raymond himself was often there, coat draped over shoulders, drink in hand. He was very likeable with a twinkle about both eyes. Nuts but likeable. Rumour had it that he owned more of London than the Queen. And Soho was Soho. Seedy but with a warm communal feel. I found I couldn't go anywhere without someone hissing from a doorway, 'Psst! Do you wanna score?' I didn't.

Back in Leeds, during the panto we had a delivery of two thousand comic books. These back issues had been sent by DC Thomson, the publisher, to be handed out to selected audience members who were invited up on stage to sing with Simple Simon, the Kiddies Friend. Between shows one afternoon, I picked up an edition of *Sparky*. It had been a favourite of mine way back in the mists of childhood, seven years ago. I found I still loved it. Especially *Hungry Horace*. Horace had been around since the thirties. A simple idea, Horace was Hungry. That was the whole basis for the strip ... and it worked. Lovable rather than greedy-guts. I enjoyed the comic so much that I started drawing and writing scripts for the established characters of the comic while hanging out backstage during the day. I gave myself a month to see if I could come up with something close enough to a professional look. At the end of that month, I bundled up four strips and sent them off to Dundee.

Three weeks went by and I just got on with my theatrical life. It was fun. It was a real escape from so-called reality. Actors create their own world where anything goes. I liked that. Every day was an adventure. To quote Gerry Anderson, anything could happen in the next half hour. You'd better stand by for action. One of the stagehands belonged to The Sealed Knot Society. He would travel the length of the country reenacting battles from the Civil War. He had the look of a gay cavalier, without the gay bit. He taught me how to sword fight up in the theatre attic. All sorts of old props and scenery became our battleground as we clashed up and down staircases, our shadows flickering across the walls. It is a wonder I still have two eyes. Two old coots playing Cinderella's Ugly Sisters fell for my curly-headed charm. They would push me into a corner backstage and lift up their crinolines to show zero underwear as they offered me £5.00 to enter their dressing room during the show's interval. No thank you. I could get five times that for writing a script. More appealing by far was Robinson Crusoe. This role was played by Pippa Boulter the daughter of John Boulter, one of the leads in *The Black & White Minstrel* Show. She told me that she didn't know whether her Dad was black or white until she turned four years of age. Pippa had blue eyes and they got me, damn them. When she bounded on stage in her leopard skin costume, smacked her fishnet stockinged thigh and declared, 'All the nice girls love a sailor', I could quite see why.

And then the letter arrived. Postmarked Dundee. I hadn't had any rejections yet so I was quite hopeful. Quite right too as it turned out because even though they rejected two of my strips, they accepted two others and suggested I pop in should I be passing Dundee. Geographically it is highly unlikely that anyone living in Leeds would pass by Dundee, but I made sure I was passing by within the week and made my first visit to the realm of DC Thomson & Co Ltd. That letter had me walking on air for several days afterwards. I can still remember just how good it made me feel. I was gonna be in the comics! *Sparky*, no less, with *Hungry Horace*.

CHAPTER 6

1972–1977

DC Thomson – Lots of Fun, For Everywun!

I liked Dundee as soon as I stepped off the train. It's one of those places that has something about it. A heartbeat. And it was Scotland. What's not to like? I found my way to Courier Place and stood for a minute looking at the DC Thomson building. It's quite a Gothic pile. It made me smile to think of all the outright naughtiness that had flown out of those office windows since the 1920s, encouraging children to be children. And now I was here to carry on that noble tradition. Children everywhere, pick up your peashooters and catapults and get revoltin'!

It was a slight letdown inside the building because there wasn't really much sign of out and out wackiness. A lot of offices and a lot of suits and a lot of people called Mr this or Mr that. A little straight after the weird and wonderful backstage world. However, it was DC Thomson and there were comic books everywhere I looked. I was met by Mr Chisholm, the editor of *Sparky*, which was a comic similar in style to the more famous *Beano* and *Dandy* weeklies. It was full of stories about naughty boys, girls, animals, and policemen. A fun read. I found out later that Mr Chisholm had been in at the birth of Dennis the Menace, even scrawling the first image on the back of a cigarette pack. He was nice and funny and one of the people in the building who I didn't have to strain to translate from the Scottish. He signed me up on the spot to produce weekly stories for *Hungry Horace*, *L Cars*, *Peter Piper*, and a new character I was to develop titled *The Adventures of a House Brick*, which was based on a house brick. I think there was a certain sixties thinking behind that idea. Mr Chisholm took me round the building to introduce me to the editors of the other titles, which brought in an unholy amount of work by the end of the week because there were a lot of weekly comics being produced at that time. *Beano*, *Dandy*, *Topper*, *Beezer*, *Buzz*, *Bunty*, *Judy*, *Hotspur*, and more. I headed back to Leeds and theatreland loaded down with comics and work. After a few months I made the decision to find a place in Dundee and attempt to work full time in comics and mags. I figured, quite rightly, that it would help keep the work coming in if I became a face rather than an envelope arriving in the editorial offices each week. The work flooded in and I found little time for anything else in my rather grotty little bedsit. The turnaround was fast and it was exciting to find my work in a variety of Thomson's publications. Not wanting to put all my eggs in one comic basket, I started writing for women's magazines and the *Sunday Post* newspaper, taking photographs and interviewing celebrities along the way. I was pretty nervous on my first interview. It was at BBC TV Centre in London with Lesley Judd, a presenter on the children's TV magazine programme *Blue Peter*. Fumbling with my tape recorder to start the interview, I accidentally opened the back panel and eight batteries fell out to roll in every direction across the *Blue Peter* office. Lesley got down on her hands and knees to retrieve the bloody things from under cupboards and desks as I found myself awash with sweat. What a nice girl, even if she did then proceed to chain-smoke roll-ups through the whole interview. She finished the interview by insisting I go out and buy Bob Dylan's *Blood on the Tracks* that minute. Good advice.

Meanwhile, back at the office I was writing a zillion strips a week. For the first couple of years I was more than happy continuing the adventures of long running characters such as *Beryl the Peril*, *Korky the Cat*, *Peter Piper*, *Tiny the World's Largest Dog*, *Mickey the Monkey*, *Danny's Tranny* (magical transistor radio in case you were wondering), *Fred the Flop*, *Ball Boy*, *Dennis the Menace*, *Bash Street Kids*, *Ginger*, *Nobby*(!), *The Four Marys*, and more. But then I had the urge to start creating more of my own characters. I kicked off with *The Tyme Twins*

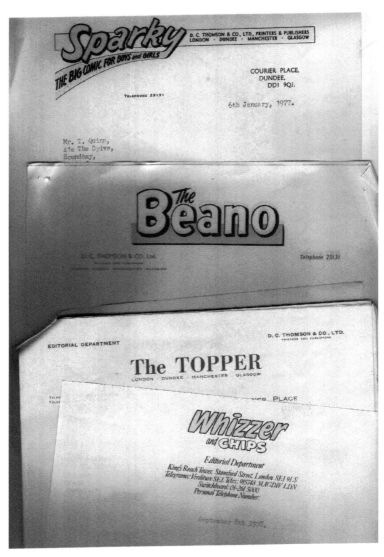

DC Thomson & Co. Ltd and IPC's Whizzer and Chips.

in *Topper*. Originally this was going to be Tim Tyme and his Dog Grimm who found Time-Hopping pogo sticks, which allowed them to have adventures through history. We were all set to go with this idea when the editor had a hiccup and told me that the readers would have a hard time suspending disbelief at a dog time traveler. He insisted that Grimm be changed to Tina, Tim's twin sister. Shame, because a dog gave a little more edge to the tales. Even so, it was fun to drop my characters into historical situations. I'd always enjoyed the adventures of *Jimmy and his Magic Patch* who was a time traveling schoolboy in the *Beano* back in the fifties. *The Tyme Twins* was a little bit sillier but still the same history. I could always look in a history book for inspiration with that strip. It was the first but by no means the last time traveling strip I would produce.

Rummaging through back issues in Thomson's morgue one lunch time, I came up with a bright idea. Over the years, the company had produced many characters whose adventures had magical or fantasy themes. My idea was to pull all of those characters together and put them in one comic. Thomson's had once run a comic weekly titled *Magic*, so that seemed the ideal name to use for my magical new periodical. I put a dummy issue together and took it to the bosses. They seemed interested. Six months later they still seemed interested. Then another six months went by where they didn't seem interested at all. Finally, as I pushed for a yes or no, I was told that the kids of today were not interested in tales of magic so we wouldn't be going with the proposal. Kids not interested in magic? This was news to me in these pre-Harry Potter days. I felt this was cobblers to put it mildly. Uh-oh, this was the start of me recognising that the management had little idea of what their audience would like. In typical if peculiar style, Thomson's went on to launch a new *Magic* comic but it was aimed at the nursery age group and full of rather wet characters.

Never mind, I was still having fun and putting a lot of work into the DC Thomson annuals of the period. Games, puzzles, stories, strips, the lot. But… something was happening. Here's a good example. I was writing a *Dennis the Menace* script for the *Beano* Christmas issue. I set the tale on Christmas Eve and had Dennis turning the house upside down in an attempt to find his presents for the next day. The editor called me in and explained that he didn't think this was a suitable idea.

'We don't want to encourage our readers to be sneaky.' I couldn't believe my ears at the time. I still can't believe it now all these years later. This was supposed to be Dennis THE MENACE! And kids are naturally sneaky when it comes to tracking down their Christmas presents before the big day. Little did I know that this was just the start. Bit-by-bit these gloriously naughty characters were being brought in to toe the line. Dennis the Menace, Beryl the Peril and Minnie the Minx were being tamed. I thought it was ridiculous that they were no longer allowed to be as naughty as they had been back in the fifties especially as the seventies were ten times more naughty. It was round about this time that I heard the phrase 'We have to be careful here' in reference to our strips not giving offense to the easily offended.

Promotional shot for DC Thomson's Tops *with Terry Wogan.*

CHAPTER 7

1978–1985

Dicky Howett and IPC

September 1978 came around with word of a convention being held down in London to mark the 101st anniversary of the birth of comic books in the UK. Sounded a good idea to me, so I booked a ticket. It was an interesting mix of people there, from Leo Baxendale (there to launch his *Willy the Kid* book) and Bill Ritchie, mainstays of old DC Thomson's to ancients such as Terry Wakefield from *Film Fun* days, and new guys Dave Gibbons and Jim Baikie. Even Western thriller author JT Edson turned up. And there, in one corner, was a man wearing a *Supermum* t-shirt. It was, who else, Dicky Howett. I knew his work because he had recently started the strip *Supermum* in *Whoopee* comic. That strip stood out a mile mainly because the other strips either looked as though they were from the 1930s or drawn by people attempting (and failing) to do a Leo Baxendale. Dicky's work was funny and highly energized. We got chatting. And then we chatted some more. We decided to see if we could come up with a few ideas as a team to rejuvenate what we felt was the rather saggy world of funny comics in the UK. Over the next few weeks we turned out a ton of material. None of which ever saw the light of day. Here are a few examples:

Fred's Family Tree – Fred was a boy with a family tree scroll from which would pop his ancestors from caveman to Victorian.

Kids' Army – *Dad's Army* but with kids set in WW2.

Olly & Stan, 'They'll Do Anything For Cash' – Two boys determined to make their fortune before leaving primary school.

Harvey's Banana – Sounds a bit dodgy but it was a simple tale about an alien who could only be seen by a boy named Harvey (shades of James Stewart). The alien was in the shape of a banana.

Cross Road – There was a popular soap at the time titled *Crossroads*. This was a tale about a road where all the inhabitants were permanently cross with each other.

Dicky and I were churning them out on top of the weekly work we already had. Thanks to him I had taken over the scripting on his Supermum character in *Whoopee*. And I got a ton more work after we went for a lunch with Bob Paynter, the Head of Humour at IPC. This was the main rival to DC Thomson's comic weeklies. Bob reminded me of Liberace in looks but his character was more Grim Reaper. His first words to me were: 'Hello, Tim. You do realise humour comics will be dead in five years?' I didn't but I could understand why the longer I worked at IPC. They were stuck in a rut and needed a good kicking. But first I signed on the line and gave them more of the same because they were much better payers than DC Thomson. Bob set me to work on titles across the line and even gave me whole annuals to script. A lot of work. *Buster*, *Whoopee*, *Whizzer & Chips*, *School Fun* (what a crap title!), and a flurry of teen mags on which I produced photo-strips, pop interviews and features.

Bob told me that he didn't think Dicky and I fit well together as a team. I disagreed. Bob did take one new strip of ours. *The Gold Rush* was about two brothers who had to take part in a marathon race round the world to determine who would win an inheritance. This got more difficult to write each week as Bob would send the script back repeatedly for changes. I noticed at one point that the script had been changed so many times that it ended up just as it had been when I first presented it. Not a lot of fun that.

CHAPTER 8

1979–1985
Marvel Comics and Adolf Hitler

So financially IPC was very handy but I felt like I was falling asleep with the type of strips they were accepting. And all the time, humour comic book sales were slipping. And then one day IPC were caught in a strike that went on for six weeks, stopping all my strip work overnight. I looked elsewhere and called Dez Skinn who was running the UK office of Marvel Comics at the time. I asked him if he would have any interest in a Quinn/Howett funny strip to slot between the super-hero strips. No. He didn't think it would work with their audience. I have to say I agreed with him on that point. However, a few weeks later I heard that Dez had left the company so I put in another call to the new Marvel UK Head, a chap called Paul Neary. He thought the idea of a Brit type funny among the super-hero strips would go down a treat and asked if we could deliver a suitable strip for a new war comic they were about to send to the printer. 'Can you get us something the day after tomorrow?' Bang! We were in. The strip was *I Was Adolf's Double* and the comic weekly was *Forces in Combat*. The story was all about a little innocent Jewish gardener who just happened to have the same face as Adolf Hitler at the worst possible time in history to have Adolf's face, World War 2. Paul changed the name of our gardener from Winston S. Cohen to Winston S. Quail for fear of offending someone somewhere. That turned out to be the only change Paul ever made to our work. As he said, he knew nothing about funny strips so he left it to us. I felt that the audience reaction would be pretty negative to our funny style popping up in a Marvel mag but I was wrong. Letters flooded in asking for more. And more we gave them. At that time, Marvel was producing about six weekly titles and four monthlies in the UK. We ended up with strips in each of them. The strips were on a variety of subjects. Ever wondered what happened to the radioactive spider that bit Peter Parker? It went on to bite Dingle Dog who became *The Fairly Amazing Spider-Hound*. In *Bullpen Bedlam* we took a look at day-to-day life in the editorial office at Marvel. *The Concise History of the Galaxy* was exactly that but without the concise bit. *Hulk the Menace* was simply Dennis meets the Hulk. A ten year-old Incredible Hulk lives with his parents in a semi somewhere in England. Instead of a peashooter in his back pocket he had an axe. Finally I could let Dennis get naughtier than ever before. *The Fantastic 400* were the world's largest super-hero group. *Earth 33⅓* was our take on Marvel's superheroes. Absurd. Ridiculous. Hey, you wander around in skintights and a cape and someone's going to laugh at some point. For all Batman's grumpiness, the world of super-heroes is pretty funny.

The relief of not having editorial changes on every strip was enormous. It made us want to do even more. We suggested a weekly funny comic for Marvel. They said, let's see a dummy issue. That dummy issue sits in front of me on my desk at this moment. It's a great comic. We brought in various comic book chums to illustrate the various stories I wrote. Geoff Campion, David Lloyd, Ron Tiner, Martin Baxendale, and, of course, Dicky Howett. It was a nice mix of funny and adventure strips. Sadly, it landed on the MD's desk at Marvel and stayed there while they lost money on an all-new girls' comic they published. After six months the decision was made to stick to reprint material on new titles. Disappointing, but we still had our weekly and monthly strips at Marvel so we couldn't complain too much. I can't say the same about things back at IPC. There was a strip called *Toy Boy*(!). Every week the main character had adventures via a new toy he would be playing with. In one script I had him playing with a toy Noah's Ark. This was returned with the line: 'We don't bring religion into our comics.' For God's sake! Dicky and I produced a strip with the nursery title *Playhour*

Dummy cover for Marvel humour comic.

in mind. It was called *Little Lost Ragga*, and was all about a little dog who got lost in the Wild West. It had humorous overtones simply because all life does. The editor of *Playhour* told me, 'Not for us. We don't deal with humour in our comic.' I've meant to get that depressing line up on a t-shirt ever since.

I was also turning in scripts for *TV Comic* at this point. This had been another favourite weekly of mine from childhood so it was fun to be on board with the strips *Popeye* and *The Inspector* (Peter Sellers character). I'd always loved Popeye and had a collection of his old strips from the thirties. I started bringing back some of the glorious old supporting characters to the strip such as the Sea Hag and the Goon. This was a lovely strip to work on. Unfortunately, early in the eighties, the comic came to an end after a thirty year life that had seen characters as diverse as *Doctor Who*, *The Telegoons*, *Coco the Clown*, *The Avengers* (Steed & Mrs Peel not Captain America & Co), *Mighty Moth*, and *Fireball XL5* grace its pages. I remember a fab free gift it once gave away during my childhood. A pack of Popeye's spinach! Can't beat that.

To promote *Supermum*, our latest Marvel strips and, most importantly, us, I contacted Rosemary Gill, the editor/producer of a Saturday morning children's BBC TV show, *Multi-Coloured Swap Shop*. I suggested we come on the show to demonstrate how comic books are made. To my surprise they thought this was a good idea and invited us in one Saturday to watch an episode going out live. Cliff Richard was the main guest that week and yes, he is as dull as you've heard. When he walked in the room I had the urge to fall asleep. Zero personality. Amazing from someone who has quite a tale to tell being in the Pop World through such amazing times but no, dull as dishwater. I blame God. Cliff was born again in the early sixties.

Anyway, even meeting us didn't put the producers off, so we were invited to make our own appearance on the show the following week. It was quite something to turn up at BBC TV Centre and head to the make-up room. They did a great job and took days off our age. The show went well, I think. Noel Edmonds, the host, was particularly good at putting us at ease. Even the presence of Adric, *Doctor Who*'s Worst Ever Companion, and Jan Leeming, the BBC's Worst Ever Newsreader, couldn't put a dampener on the buzz we got from broadcasting to the nation. I felt we were great, naturals. Best bit was when I got the tube back into central London from White City. As I walked up into Oxford Street, a guy did a double-take and said, 'Hey, you were on TV this morning!' I'd arrived! It's just a shame then that Dicky videoed the show so we could watch it later. Oh dear. Me. Awful. I would still cringe today if I had to watch it even though I am several lifetimes on. Talk about a learning curve. Ick!

Multi-Coloured Quinn & Howett deal or no deal.

So there we were working for Marvel UK. What fun. So many weeklies and monthlies, and *Doctor Who Magazine*. Memory is a bit blurry on the exact detail but I think it was editor Alan McKenzie who brought us in for that. I seem to remember that we had already done a *Doctor Who* spoof strip for another publisher but it hadn't been used. Why *Doctor Who*? Mainly because there was no magazine based on Garry Halliday, my other favourite Saturday night viewing. No, I'm being silly (although, what a great idea!). Dicky was as into *Doctor Who* as I was so it came very naturally to create a spoof version. Spoof, yes, but spoofed with love. And by the time we got into the swing and created this odd *Who?* world that mixed the six or seven Doctors with their actor counterparts and BBC TV Centre with dimensions in time and space, we had enormous fun with the strip.

We even started being invited to *Doctor Who* conventions. This was our first close encounter with *Doctor Who* fans of the third kind.

> Fan: 'You know in last January's issue you had the Doctor say blah-di-blah-de-blah?'
>
> Me: 'Er... yes?'
>
> Fan: 'Well this contradicts what the Doctor said in episode three of *The Web Planet* back in 1965.'

Welcome to the World of Fandom. We fit in quite well actually and it set me up for later dealings with fans of Sherlock Holmes when I did a few Conan Doyle adaptations and similar scenes would be re-enacted.

My first years in the US were enlivened by the Whosier Network, a group of fans in Indianapolis who met on the first Friday of every month to chat and view old *Doctor Who* episodes. They gave brilliant support to the local PBS station that was running the series at that time. I found myself roped in during pledge drives at the station to encourage viewers to send in cash donations to keep PBS running. Somewhere on YouTube is film of me auctioning off four bales of hay. Hey, it was Indiana, a big farming area.

Meanwhile back at Marvel UK, *DWM* editors came and went. Surprisingly our strip remained a constant feature of the mag, even getting the odd full page extra space now and again. I should stress now that we loved all the editors apart from whoever eventually dropped us. Actually, maybe we dropped ourselves; again a blurring of the memory fluid links. And we certainly loved all the actors we met from the series. Oh, I do remember that I did piss Sarah Sutton off at one point. There was a *Doctor Who* tour crossing the US and they pitched up at Channel 20 in Indianapolis for a two-day meet-and-greet. I was invited along by the station to sign copies of our just released *Doctor Who Fun Book* from Target and WH Allen. On the first day I sidled up to Sarah and got a lovely photo of the pair of us with me strategically doing the product placement of the *Fun Book* centre frame. That night I got one hundred copies of the photo developed and took them along the following day to sign for the fans. As I was giving them away, they went down like hot cakes until Sarah was asked to sign one. As she was flogging her photos, this was seen as a hostile act on my part. I was warned to desist at once or face the wrath of the BBC. Not since the ice cream wars of the Eighties has there been such tension. Never mind. Always preferred Adric myself.

Scarer Sutton.

Bigger on the Inside was almost a lot smaller on the inside. We had spoken with Marvel about doing it as a follow up to the *Fun Book* for about two years. Typically, when they said yes they gave us a deadline of mere weeks. At that time I was moving house and dashing between the US and UK, so the book was written on trains and planes but mostly in waiting rooms waiting for trains and planes. To get ahead I even pulled photos from a Quinn family album to drop into a chapter on *Doctor Who*'s Photo Album. Cheat!

Doctor Who. The words still get me. No matter what has happened since 1963, I immediately see William Hartnell when I hear the programme mentioned. The ten year old boy is now older than William Hartnell was when he played the role. How'd that happen? The mysteries of time. It was enormous fun to bring the Doctor and Ian to life for a *Doctor Who Yearbook* in a straight tale. The story kicks off with them just chatting about the wonders of the universe. I loved that kind of thing in the early years of the show. Leaping into the unknown every Saturday. The Vortis studio set is exactly how I want distant planets to look. All that and history too without an alien in sight (unless you count the Meddling Monk, and the Daleks on the Marie Celeste). Those early adventures have yet to let go.

Quinn & Howett acting.

And so the weeks and months and years clicked by. Dicky and I suddenly realised that due to our weekly workload we had turned out a hell of a lot of strips for Marvel. We suggested collecting many of them together as a Summer Special type title to test the water for attempting to produce a new humour weekly. There was a new MD at Marvel UK by this time so why not hit him with an old idea. He agreed that if the collection sold well then we could look at doing a weekly. And so we set out on a promotional trail to ensure that the Great British public were aware that *Channel 33⅓ The Children's Comic* was hitting the stands. We were in local press, on local radio and TV news programmes. It really must have been a slow news year because we got ourselves on everything. Consequently the comic sold very well for a one-off type publication. Wahoo! Looked as if we were going to get our weekly after all this time. But life's not like that, is it? We had a great response from everybody who picked up *Channel*. Everybody that is except one person. A Dad. An angry Dad. A very angry Dad. He was so angry he sent a copy of the comic to his local paper claiming it was disgusting and full of mass murder, glue sniffing, prostitution, and copulation. In our defense I have to say this isn't true. The comic wasn't full of these subjects. We merely touched upon them in some of the stories. Kids didn't have a problem. Nor did all the rest of the parents in the land. The newspaper decided to build a story round this Dad's rage under the headline: Anger Over Comic Smut. Look, Mum, I'm in the papers! The newspaper said it had done the decent thing and passed the comic book on to the DPP (Department of Public Prosecutions). Instead of saying bollocks to this, Marvel decided to drop us from all their mags except *Doctor Who Monthly*. 'Just until the heat dies down.' It took six months for the DPP to report that they could find nothing wrong with the comic, and by then Marvel had moved on. Bugger! Bugger! Bugger!

In retrospect this wasn't such a bugger after all. It made me move on. Viz was my first call. They couldn't have cared less that I was under investigation by the police. In their eyes it was a positive bonus. And Viz was funny… back then. I also put in a call to the *Daily Mirror*'s Strips Dept. As luck would have it, I called at just the right moment and was given the scripting duty on their long running strip Jane. Created back in the thirties, the main character was a 'bright young thing' who just happened to lose her clothes twice a week during each adventure. Sounds a little odd now but I was very pleased to be taking over such a historic strip.

I also mailed out the dummy of the humour comic we had put together for Marvel to Terry Jones of *Monty Python*. I had heard him mention his love of old comic books in a radio interview. A few weeks later I heard back from Terry in a well thought out critique of the comic. He liked most of the pages though told me that his young daughter loved every page. He offered to send £500 to help with getting the comic up and running. Very kind but at that point I had little idea on how to raise the rest. Terry also gave me the contact details to meet up with his friend Gilbert Shelton, the underground artist of the *Furry Freak Brothers*. The meeting went ahead in a mews in Chelsea, and very enjoyable it was too but our styles were too far apart to make sense of a team-up via Gilbert's publishing company.

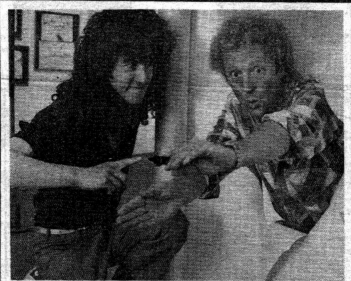

Pow! — cartoon partners Tim Quinn, left, and Dicky Howett

The cartoon characters

THE zany Scouser who lives in a bubble is back in Liverpool.

And Tim Quinn told the Echo of the days he spent eating cow pies with Desperate Dan and of how he came to fall in love with Minnie the Minx. *Lies!*

Tim fills in the bubbles for some of the nation's favourite comic strip characters.

He is at the Bluecoat Chambers with artist and partner Dicky Howett to show how cartoons are made.

Tim, 32, who was brought up in Crosby confessed: "I have become something of a cartoon character myself. In this day and age it is the best way to behave."

At the moment his big obsession is the voluptuous wartime cartoon beauty Jane. He has just got the contract to write her scripts for the Daily Mirror.

Tim said: "I have always been one of her greatest fans — I can't wait to get to work on her." *True!!*

His early days were spent working for the Beano and the Dandy and he says he made many friends there.

"I used to hang about with the Bash Street Kids and I was one of Lord Snooty's pals. But the great love of my life was Minnie the Minx." *Rubbish!*

And in an exclusive interview with the Echo, Minnie said: "Tim was the greatest. When he was with me I used to say the most incredible things."

Natural pose.

46

Jane *of the* Daily Mirror.

CHAPTER 9

1986
Jane

Feeling a little gloomy that I was back to square one in humour comics, I picked up a copy of the latest edition of *The Beatles Book*. This was a monthly publication I'd bought since August 1963. By the eighties the price had risen dramatically and I remember making the decision that this would be the final issue I'd buy. Flicking through I found an advert from a woman in the US who asked if anyone in the UK would like to swap houses for the summer. Seemed like a good idea to me, so I wrote to her. By coincidence her name was Jane. And she wrote back. And I wrote back to her. And then she wrote back to me. Soon it became obvious we weren't talking houses. And so we met three months later, at Heathrow at 7:00am. My first word to Jane was: 'Hoi!' as she walked past me, not yet used to British-sized short-arse people. We saw the sights of Liverpool, York, Southport, Leeds and London in the two weeks she was over here. On the final day we knew this was it. Love. And so we made plans that I would sort out a few outstanding work projects here in the UK and then move over to join her in Indianapolis.

Before I left, I mailed out an idea Dicky and I had put together for a birthday book to Sid Jacobson at Star Comics, the Marvel junior imprint of the time. Sid had been brought over to Marvel from Harvey

Comics to launch the line. We claimed our book was the perfect extra gift for aunts, uncles, parents and grandparents to buy for little Tommy and Tina on their birthdays. Sid wrote me a very nice letter back saying how much he liked the proposal and execution, and inviting me to drop by if I found myself in New York. And so it was that I found myself in New York one sweltering summer's day, on my way to Indiana. Lugging an overweight shoulder bag with all my worldly clothes, I staggered into the Marvel Comics office for the first time. What an exciting place to find myself on my first day in NYC! Sid was great too. While he couldn't get Marvel or Star to invest in our birthday book he suggested I try scripting some of the Star line of characters. Not a bad first day in the US.

And then I fell in love. Jane.

Sat Evening Post *kids' mag*

Sat Evening Post *kids' mag*

CHAPTER 10

1986–1991
USA – The Saturday Evening Post Magazine

And arriving in Indianapolis, things got better with each passing day. I flipped through the local *Yellow Pages* under Publishers and found to my surprise that *The Saturday Evening Post Magazine* was based in town. The *Post* had been created by Ben Franklin back in the 1720s, and some of the best writers and illustrators had worked on the magazine ever since. F Scott Fitzgerald and PG Wodehouse to name but two. I phoned the editorial office and rather oddly was put through to the publisher herself. I explained my work in comics and cartoons in the UK and said I hoped to sell cartoons to the *Post*. She suggested I come into the office. I asked when would be a good time and she barked: 'Now!' Well, that was different from how things worked in the UK. In Britain you'd make an appointment for weeks ahead, and you wouldn't get in to see the publisher but rather be fobbed off on some lowly editor.

Arriving at Waterway Blvd., I was shown into the publisher's office. Her name was Cory SerVaas, a tiny woman who was wearing a doctor's lab coat complete with stethoscope hanging round her neck. I handed her my portfolio of ghastly cartoons. She flipped through quickly and handed it back saying, 'I don't know anything about humour.' I was soon to find out just how true that statement was. 'Whereabouts in England are you from?' she asked. 'Liverpool' I replied. Everything stopped. She stared at me with a look of wonder in her eyes. 'Liverpool? You're from Liverpool?' I smiled and nodded in agreement. 'How'd you like to start work on Monday?' she responded. I was taken aback. I'd only gone in to sell a cartoon. 'Doing what?' I asked. She thought for a moment before declaring, 'You can be our Humor Editor. You guys are supposed to be funny from Liverpool, aren't you?' I could hardly deny that fact. I wandered out to the car where Jane waited patiently. 'Did you sell a cartoon?' she asked. 'I've got a job!' I replied. 'How much?' asked the American. I dashed back inside the office to find out. Amazing. In a single bound I had gone from the *Beano* to one of America's most sophisticated magazines. Great Scott! as they say in the comics. Was I nervous? You betcha. I mean, I'd never been a Humor Editor before. Turned out that nobody else had been either. This was a brand new position created on the spot.

Humor Editor waves flag humorously.

The following Monday as I entered the *Post*'s reception, Cory hurried over to me and told me to wait there. 'I have to go and fire someone to make way for you.' Welcome to USA business style. Half an hour passed when a disgruntled former employee walked from the editorial office, carrying a cardboard box full of folders, stationary and a framed photo of his family. 'Are you the British guy?' he asked. I nodded. 'Well good luck, bud. You'll need it.' Not much of a welcoming committee. After he had departed to shoot himself, Cory returned and walked me

The portrait on my office wall at The Saturday Evening Post Magazine.

down several corridors to my new office. Someone was already taking the old name off the door and putting up a nameplate with the legend 'TIM QUINN – HUMOR EDITOR'. I had arrived.

Hanging on the wall behind my desk was a huge portrait of Richard Nixon. It somehow seemed apt that of all the presidents, he was the one on my office wall. 'First thing I want you to do,' said Cory as I settled in my swivel chair, 'is to put together a book about AIDS for children. Do not mention homosexuals. I know I can trust you because I've met your wife.' With that she turned and walked out of the office. I swiveled and looked up at Tricky Dicky. The word 'huh?' came to mind. I mean, HUH?!

The office wall was paper thin. I could overhear someone in the next office having a phone conversation. 'Yeah, apparently he's English. And now he's our Humor Editor. How can an Englishman know anything about American humor?' Bloody cheek, I thought. I'd watched *Mr Ed* and *My Mother the Car*. But AIDS? This was in the early days of the disease. Nobody knew much about it, and everybody walked in fear of the word. I didn't want to know about it. I did know it had nothing to do with humor or even humour. One thing I found out that first day was that the *Post* also ran seven children's magazines. Several of them had been running for decades and were a big part of American life. *Jack & Jill*, *Humpty Dumpty*, *Child Life*, *Children's Digest*, *Turtle*, *Children's Playmate*, and *Stork*. None of them had any strips so I told each editor that I would create a new strip for their particular mag. I had started work on this by midday when Cory came back into my office and asked how the AIDS book was coming along. 'Erm… I'm just turning ideas of best approach over in my head while working up strips for the kids' mags,' I babbled. 'Well, hurry up,' she barked. 'People are dying!' Off she went again leaving me more bewildered than before. Was I supposed to come up with a cure now?

It was an interesting building I found myself in. Norman Rockwell originals lined the corridor walls and there was a display case of Benjamin Franklin's nik-naks outside my office door. One thing became clear as I met more of my fellow editors. Everybody walked in fear of the boss. On my second day in the job I saw a grown man hide behind his office door when Cory came storming down the corridor. She seemed to be angry quite a lot. But not with me. After many hours

Los Angeles Times

SUNDAY MORNING, JANUARY 31, 1988/PRICE: ONE DOLLAR

Getting the Word Out

The Saturday Evening Post is collecting material (poems, writings, photos) for a book on AIDS from most unlikely contributors who, so far, include Yoko Ono, Harlan Ellison, Isaac Asimov, Hugh Hefner, Elton John, Gene Wilder and Dan Aykroyd. Cartoonists and artists have also signed on, including "Beetle Bailey's" Mort Walker and "Doonesbury's" Garry Trudeau.

Profit would go to the magazine's AIDS information program. Post publisher Cory Ser Vaas serves on the President's Commission on AIDS and the magazine sponsors an AIDS-mobile that travels the country dispensing information on the disease. Contributions from celebrities are being accepted until March 7.

According to Post humor editor Tim Quinn, who's editing the book, it will include "almost any-. thing"—cartoon strips, poems, stories, photos and sketches, plus easily digested and basic information about the disease, aimed at readers who ordinarily might not read about it.

Ellison, Quinn said, "wrote a wonderful story." Ono "sent a typical Yoko poem, very warm and loving." Archie Comics is sending pages depicting their characters in class while a teacher discusses AIDS. Asimov wrote what Quinn described as a "very strange piece about why it is called AIDS . . . why just those four letters."

Does Quinn fear trivializing the subject by having entertainers and non-authorities address it?

"It cannot be trivialized," he insisted. "The idea is to bring it home to as many people as possible."

— *From Matthew Costello in NYC*

()

LA Times.

MARVEL PRODUCTIONS LTD.
6007 SEPULVEDA BLVD.
VAN NUYS, CALIFORNIA 91411
(818) 988-6300 • TELEX #182325

STAN LEE

1/18/88

Mr. Tim Quinn
Humour Editor
The Saturday Evening Post
1100 Waterway Blvd.
Indianapolis
Indiana 46202

Dear Tim,

Thanks for your letter of 1/5 clarifying what you're looking for
in regards to the book you're doing for children relative to the
AIDS situation. (Wow! Talk about convoluted sentences!)

I was really stuck for an idea as to what to write, since I can't
think of too many humorous things to say about AIDS. Finally, I
resorted to a device I've often used when I had to write a column
for our comics-- I'd put my little message in the form of a poem.
I thought perhaps a simple verse that had some bearing on the
problem might do the trick for you now. And, after you read the
attached bit of poesy, you'll see why I'm known as a comicstrip
writer rather than poet laureate!

Anyway, I hope it'll serve the purpose. I'm also accompanying it
with a bit of artwork which you're free to use or not depending
on how it strikes you.

I trust this will prove satisfactory to you. If not, there's
time enough for you to let me know and perhaps I can come up with
something else.

Wishing you much luck with your project...

Cordially,

Stan

P.S. Be sure to send me a copy of the book when it's published,
or I'll send The Hulk after ya!

A NEW WORLD COMPANY

Stan the Man.

58

of staring at a blank wall I'd hit upon a way to get the AIDS book up and running. My plan was to ask celebrities to mail in… anything. A poem, a drawing, a photo, a short story, absolutely anything; it didn't even have to have anything to do with AIDS. I would place each celebrity's work on a page in the book and write a simple fact about the disease underneath it. My aim was to attempt to get rid of the stigma that was attached to the very word AIDS by showing that names in the public eye were supportive of sufferers. At this point in time the only celebrity who had his name linked with AIDS was Rock Hudson, and that was because he had the disease rather than that he was supporting people who had it. Of course, I didn't know if anyone would actually want their name attached to the disease. Regardless, I mailed off letters to the few celebrity names whose addresses I could track down. Three days later, my office phone rang. 'Is that Tim Quinn?' asked a very recognisable voice. 'This is Yoko Ono. I'd like to help with your AIDS project.' I was in business. I put in a call to the editor of the *Los Angeles Times*. Thanks to Yoko we got a front page story putting the word out that I was seeking celebs to help with the book. Over the next two months I was inundated with material from the biggest names of the period. Jane Fonda, the cast of *Cheers*, Gene Wilder, Charlton Heston, Joan Baez, Elton John, Hugh Hefner, the Pope, Dan Aykroyd, Mort Walker, Gary Trudeau, Phyllis Diller, to name but a few. Yes, THE Pope! Actually he sent a letter on Vatican stationary that ran along the lines of, 'I wish you well with your AIDS book, unfortunately I cannot contribute myself.' Ha-hah! thought I. You just have. So I got out my White Out and very carefully got rid of the 'unfortunately' line. That would do nicely as a greeting. But where to put the Pope's page in the book? I decided to put him face-to-face with Hugh Hefner's contribution, which was a cartoon drawing of himself. Talk about both ends of the sexual spectrum.

And then I got a very nice letter from Stan Lee at Marvel Comics. He wanted to contribute to the book using his Spider-Man character and also writing a piece of poetry calling for acceptance for people who had the disease. Thanks, Stan. During one of many phone conversations it turned out that Stan was a big fan of the *Jane* comic strip I was still writing for the Daily Mirror back in the UK. Holy cow! Stan knew my stuff! Now he was on board I headed over to DC to enlist

Superman and Batman to the AIDS book. The company signed on as soon as they heard that Stan had contributed. So did Archie Comics. The book was turning into an extraordinary piece of work. *Rolling Stone* magazine rang to do an interview about the project. By now I saw the worth of the book. The timing was perfect and I do believe it helped in a tiny way to shatter the stupid stigma attached to the word AIDS. And it helped me to leap out of the comic book box I had created round myself.

The Humor Editor at The Saturday Evening Post Magazine *working on his AIDS book.*

Even so, this was a strange new world I was working in. One day I was called into a Very Important Meeting with the heads of Kelloggs. They had a dilemma. Kids weren't eating All Bran. Cory thought as a person of humour I might be able to come up with fun reasons to get the children of America to put aside their marshmallow and chocolate morning cereals in favour of eating tree bark. She must be joking. Of course, she wasn't. Another time she asked me to come up with several cartoons to turn young people against taking snuff. I hadn't realised this was a problem since the Regency but Cory informed me that it was growing to epidemic proportions across the US with children burning holes in their heads through this particular substance abuse. I drew up a cartoon of a guy with a hole in his head and the caption: 'You need snuff like a hole in the head.' Hilarious. I was cornering the Disease & Illness Cartoon Market.

You never knew who would be visiting the *Post* from day to day. Looking up from my work on one bright morning, I saw President Reagan walking by accompanied by a squad of security agents all in dark glasses. Later that same day, fifties crooner Pat Boone knocked on my office door. He had heard that I had connections to Stan Lee at Marvel Comics. 'I have a great idea for a Marvel Comic,' he told me. 'A team of handicapped super-heroes. They all have a handicap but they all also have a super-power. Do you think Stan would be interested in this?' I told him it sounded more suitable for a British comic magazine called *Viz*. While ignoring Pat Boone's wonderful creation I went time traveling again myself with a new slant on the travel side. My new creation was Tim Tyme for the *Post*'s *Children's Digest* magazine. He had a new look and a new mode of transport. This time Tim soared through American history on a skateboard. The strip ran for fifteen years and is a favourite of mine to this day.

I must say that the *Post* was a strange place to work. This was mainly down to our Boss Lady. I would arrive for work most mornings to find a stack of memos from her that had been delivered through the night. A typical memo ran: 'Tiny Tim, I want you to encourage our readers to donate their body parts after death. Can you start by drawing a cartoon showing a gangster type lurking in the shadows with a cigarette hanging from his lips like a flaccid penis. Go on to show how smoking can hurt the organs so that they are useless for redistribution after death.' Believe me, that was a typical memo. The Humor Editor had his work cut out for him. I enjoyed creating new strips for each of the *Post*'s seven children's mags. But even here Cory insisted that there would be health related topics on at least eighteen pages of a forty-eight-page publication. She wanted my strips to also feature healthy issues. I got round this with one strip by collaborating with Dicky Howett on an all-new version of *The Fantastic 400*. This time round they were called *The Fitness 400*. Happily, Cory only read the title and was appeased that I was following her direction. In fact the strips were as batty as any we'd done for Marvel.

The Celebrity AIDS Book

A Preview

by Andy Mangels

Fast on the paperback heels of *Strip AIDS USA* comes another "jam" book to benefit AIDS foundations. This one, *the Celebrity AIDS Book*, is being spear-headed by the *Saturday Evening Post*.

Unlike its two comic book predecessors, *The Celebrity AIDS Book* unites artists and celebrities from all of the arts: Movies, TV, Comic Books, Music, Dance, Comic Strips, Politics, and several "real world," non-celebrity people.

Tim Quinn, humor editor at the *Saturday Evening Post*, is editing the book, a position about which he at first felt very odd. "We have several children's magazines here at the *Post*," says Quinn, "including *Jack and Jill*, *Humpty Dumpty*, and *Child's Life*. We run letter's columns for the kids, including a doctor's column. We kept getting lots of letters from kids saying 'Look, what's this AIDS? We've heard about it, but our parents won't tell us what it is, and we want to know about it.'"

Cory SerVaas, publisher of the *Post*, then came to Quinn and asked him to do an AIDS-related book—one which would get all of the facts across to kids (defined here as "early teens to late teens"). "I thought 'Oh God,'" says Quinn, "I don't want to do that. I don't know the first thing about it, and I'm the humor editor for goodness sake! I thought about it for a while, and came up with something that I would want to read myself."

Quinn then read several AIDS-related books, knowing nothing about the disease "other than the 'fact' that if you meet somebody with AIDS you're supposed to be scared. I started reading several long, dull, boring books on AIDS, which at least limited my ignorance on that matter. These

were the kinds of books that if you gave them to a teenager, they wouldn't get past the first paragraph."

Quinn had been involved with *Food For Thought* in England in 1985. *Food For Thought* was a famine-relief book, the proceeds of which benefitted Bob Geldof's *Live Aid* program. "We had asked all of the top British cartoonists to contribute a page to the magazine. Some of them did strips about Ethiopia, while others of them just did humorous strips. In the end, we had a wonderful magazine. It sold for a pound, and we sold over a million copies in England alone!"

While the format and structure of *Food For Thought* were acceptable for what Quinn wanted to do with the AIDS book, he did not want to rely solely on the cartoonists of the country. "I like cartoonists, and I know cartoonists, but the majority of

the general public can't tell one cartoonist from another. So I thought 'Right, we'll get the greatest cartoonists I can find, but we'll open it up a little and see if celebrities will come in on the book as well. Writers, actors, anybody who is anybody. My idea was that the only way to sell a book with the word AIDS in the title, was to make it very commercial."

After tracking down many phone numbers and addresses, Quinn sent many "celebrities" a simple letter, telling them that the *Post* was putting together a book which featured comic strips, cartoons, photos, poems, sketches, stories, and even simple messages. These would be combined with easily understood facts about the disease. "The facts would be extremely simple," says Quinn, "because I knew we would be selling the book to teenagers, and as soon as they came to a whole pile of facts, they would not read it. My ideas is almost subliminal; on each page there is a fact, but they are so short and to-the-point, that it will almost go into their head without reading it."

Quinn did not specifically ask for material on AIDS, as he imagined that most of the people might know as little about AIDS as he had when he started the project. "As editor of the book, the commercial side of me was looking for names that I could highlight on the cover, so that people would buy the book for the names, regardless of the fact that it was about AIDS. I thought that it would be an education in and of itself, to see that these well-known people were not afraid to have their name linked to that word."

As Quinn had expected, there was a big difference in how people responded to contributing to a book about AIDS, as opposed [to] a book about the starving people in Ethiopia. Public conscience only goes so far

Joan Baez contributed her talent (and name) to help victims of the AIDS virus.

AIDS Celebrity Book.

Trina Robbins (with Max and Mo) fights the general ignorance about AIDS.

One person contacted Quinn about doing a piece for the book, even though she was not a celebrity. "Her brother died of AIDS, and she wanted to write about the effect it had on her and her family. There were some absolutely beautiful things that really brought some of these people together on this project. I was surprised that several people *did* write about *their* personal feeling towards AIDS. Many of the celebrities have allowed their name to be linked to the word AIDS, even though some of their agents didn't particularly like that."

Quinn continues. "All of the people who took their time and energy to do this book are wonderful, wonderful people. When I was first approached to do this, my mind said 'Oh dear, this isn't going to be much fun. The subject and everything about it will be grim to say the least.' Actually, it has turned out to be a wonderful project. The collection of names is so diverse, that there will be something in there for everyone. It's the kind of magazine I would want to buy, because it is *so* different."

The Celebrity AIDS Book will be published magazine-sized, in a square-bound format. Because the *Post* is still receiving submissions, they are unsure of the page count, although it will be somewhere between 60 and 100 pages in length, with full-color on most pages. The price will be kept as low as possible, to encourage more people to buy it. Publication will be in early September, with nationwide media coverage.

All proceeds from *The Celebrity AIDS Book* will go towards further AIDS education—especially education aimed at children.

Cory SerVaas, the *Post*'s publisher is on the *President's AIDS Commission*, and the *Post* runs an AIDSmobile. The AIDSmobile is a van which travels around the country with a crew of doctors, stopping in various towns and spreading information about AIDS and its prevention. "You can see that *The Celebrity AIDS Book* is not the only thing that the *Post* does to help combat ignorance about AIDS," says Quinn.

"One of the things I really hope to do with the book," concludes Quinn, "is help to remove the stigma from the word AIDS. It is just a disease, not a social disease or a God-sent disease or a gay disease. It is a 'people disease.' Again, we're trying to remove the stigma surrounding the word AIDS. If we can help get around people's reaction to that word, we will have done some good." ●

ANDY MANGELS is a sometime reviewer for *Amazing Heroes* (see this issue, page 71).

before uncomfortableness and ignornace begin taking a firmer hold. "Thankfully, the majority—the vast majority—were only too willing to do something. Many of them called me up immediately, saying that they were proud to do something to help. Not only did they say that, but then they followed through! I had the material from them on my desk within a week! That's amazing in magazines, because the hardest thing for an editor is to get people to stick to a deadline. In this case, where they were not getting paid or aything, it was wonderful! It's quite amazing. I think a year ago, this might not have happened so easily, but people are becoming more informed."

Yoko Ono (wife of the late Beatle, John Lennon) was one of the first people to respond, providing Quinn with leverage and a "big name" to bring other people onto the project. The line-up of the book includes: Stan Lee (Marvel Comics), Garry Trudeau (*Doonesbury*), the DC Comics staff (a ten-page strip using their popular heroes), Isaac Asimov, Spider-Man, Harlan Ellison, Hugh Hefner, Mr. Rogers, Mindy Newell (*Lois Lane, Catwoman*), Mort Walker (*Beetle Bailey*), Dan Akroyd, Carol Burnett, Sylvester McCoy (*Dr. Who*), Joan Baez, Ed Asner, Dicky Howett (Britian's top children's artist), Stacey Keach, the Djubugay tribe (an Australian Aborigne tribe), Trina Robbins and the *California Girls*, Mike McCartney (Paul's brother), Phyllis Diller, Charlton Heston, Mary Engelbreit (top-selling greeting card artist in America), Miss America, Charles Bronson, Jill Ireland, Ted Danson, Kirstie Allie, Rodney Dangerfield, sometimes *Amazing Heroes* scribe Andy Mangels, who will be doing a comic story with an as yet unnamed artist, and many others.

AUGUST/SEPTEMBER1988

Children's Digest®

What Happened in 1769? Find Out With Tim Tyme!

Another Quinn Time Traveller.

CHAPTER 11

1988

National Periodicals – DC Comics

Ever since Dicky and my aborted *Beano* style comic for Marvel UK, I'd been sending the dummy round to the odd publisher but always with zero luck. Chatting on the phone with Paul Levitz at *Superman*'s DC Comics one day regarding the AIDS project, I asked if DC had any interest in humour comics. He told me that it was something they kicked around in editorial meetings every so often but that they hadn't come up with a suitable project yet. He suggested I meet up with one of his editors next time I was in New York. And so the following week I found myself sitting next to a dummy of Clark Kent in the DC reception. Mike Gold was the editor and we had a very pleasant afternoon and evening talking all things humour. The question was asked: would a *Beano* style comic work in the US? The management at DC deliberated over this point for the next month before coming to the conclusion that no, it wouldn't. Oh well, never mind. Put the kettle on.

And then, sitting in my office at the *Post* one afternoon, I get two quite separate calls from England. The first was from a journalist named Don Short. Don was one of the main reporters who covered the Beatles stories during their touring years. We had met somewhere, some time. He was now running a syndication agency supplying features to publishers around the world. Don told me that he was in talks

February 26, 1988

Mr. Tim Quinn
Humour Editor
The Saturday Evening Post
1100 Waterway Boulevard
Indianapolis, IN 46202

Dear Tim:

Thanks for the material on the AIDS book, which I personally transferred
to Chantal d'Aulnis (our Director of Business Affairs & International)
for follow up. Sorry for letting it get mislaid the first time out.

As to the humor idea, we have a lot of desire to do comics for kids, and
great pessimism as to the possibility of distributing them well enough
to sell a decent run. Why don't you let me know next time you're coming
into New York, and I'll set up a lunch for us with one of our senior
editors who's equally fascinated with the problem. Maybe the two of you
can get some ideas going.

Best,

Paul Levitz

American humor.

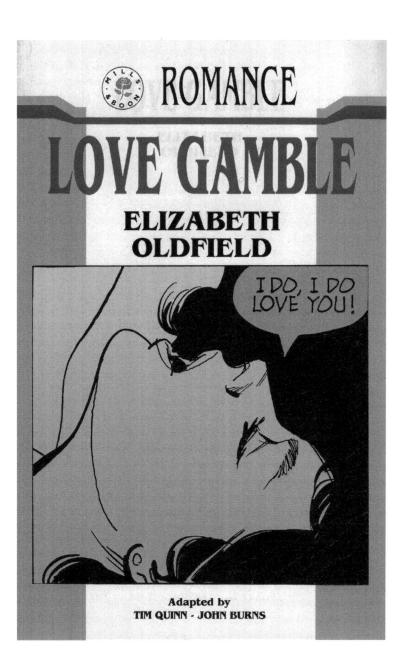

Romance!

with Guinness to produce a comic book spin-off to their *World Records* book. Would I be interested in editing such a publication? I assured him I might well be. Putting the phone down it immediately rang again. This time it was John Brown, the publisher of *Viz*. I'd met John years before when he was running Pete Townshend's publishing company, Eel Pie Publishing. John told me that he was looking at the possibility of creating a junior *Viz* style comic. Would I be interested in putting a dummy together? Yes. What a day! Both very exciting projects and each with a hugely successful company behind it. What could possibly go wrong? Ha! This is the publishing world.

Actually, nothing went wrong. For ages. There were pages created and sent and meetings held. And weeks turned into months turned into years. And then, just as we were about to go with Guinness, new management stepped in and all present projects were canned. Meanwhile, over at *Viz*, goodness knows how many *Viz* rip-offs were now hitting the newsstands each month. A lot. All missing that one vital ingredient that made *Viz* work. They weren't funny. John Brown decided that the market was too cluttered to produce yet another *Viz*-style comic although he did want to buy the latest version of *The Fantastic 400* off me. I decided to hold onto it. I'm still holding onto it today. Ho-hum.

While working at the *Post* I was also creating strips for any number of magazines back in the UK. It was a time when editors still recognized that a regular strip would help add personality to their publication. It was easy enough to fashion strips after the general theme of each mag. Casting my net further I made contact with Mills & Boon, the romance publishers. I suggested they might bring in a teen audience if their books were adapted to the growing graphic novel format. They bought this premise and sent me ten books to choose the first adaptation from. I read one and then the next and the next and the next before realising they were all much the same so threw them all in the air and caught the winner. Somehow word of this venture got out and I was contacted by the editor of the *Sun* newspaper who told me he wanted to sex up his paper with a strip based on a Mills & Boon book. Obviously he had never read any of their books. Together with master illustrator John M. Burns I got to work on the adaptations. Fun in a can't-believe-I'm-doing-this kind of way. Despite a big launch with a full page of the strip, it soon became obvious that sexy wasn't exactly a staple of Mills & Boon storylines. Three weeks in I got a call from editor Kelvin at the *Sun*. He came right to the point. 'When's the sex start?' I explained that M&B were more into Romance. He made a noise down the phoneline that went something like 'Pfffff!' And that was it. The strip was dropped in mid story the very next day. Shame because it was very well paid as newspaper strips were in those days. Over at the *Daily Mirror* I had come up with the idea of introducing real life characters into the *Garth* strip. The current story featured rock legend Tina Turner as Garth's girlfriend. Tina gave me a great quote about her appearance in the strip. 'This is better than getting the cover of *Vogue*.' The *Mirror* splashed the quote over a two-page spread at the start of that particular story.

Quinn script for Garth *in the* Daily Mirror.

CHAPTER 12

1991–1992
Sherlock Holmes

A project of sheer joy at this time was working with Gyles Brandreth to turn out three comic book adaptations of Sherlock Holmes stories. How to describe Gyles? He is Gyles Brandreth and I love him dearly. He should be running Great Britain, even his initials fit. Anyway, I'd met him years earlier and it turned out we both had a love of all things Conan Doyle. Among a thousand other jobs, he was running an editorial packaging company called Complete Editions. He sold the idea of Holmes in comic strip format to Collins Books and we were away. We chose the stories *The Hound of the Baskervilles*, *The Speckled Band*, and *The Blue Carbuncle*. I wanted to give the books a *Tintin* feel so chose the American illustrator George Sears to supply the artwork. I traveled round Britain to promote them on the week leading up to their launch. I found that local radio and TV news was only interested in stories that were grounded locally. To get over this I claimed in each area that the background illustrations were based on buildings in each town. Nonsense, of course, but it got me on each programme.

Gyles Brandreth. The game is afoot.

Sherlock books.

Sherlock Holmes books promotion for TV news.

CHAPTER 13

1992–1995
Marvel Comics again

While in London for a meeting with the Strips Dept at the *Daily Mirror* I had heard that Marvel UK was expanding in a big way. They were churning out a ton of brand new work to launch over in the US, and they were looking for editorial staff. Interesting. Back at the *Post* in Indianapolis I was called into the publisher's office one day soon after this UK trip. Cory told me that she had received a letter of complaint about one of the stories I'd written for *Jack & Jill* magazine. She handed me the letter. It was postmarked Alabama. Alarm bells immediately. It was from the mother of a regular reader of *Jack & Jill* and began in the time honoured way of letters of complaint with the words: 'Dear Editor, I was disgusted…' She was disgusted to find that my story featured an elf living in a tree house with a robin. Or, as the mother put it, 'co-habiting'. I laughed out loud as I read the letter and asked if I should file it under wastepaper basket. But Cory was not amused. 'We must take this seriously. This is one of our subscribers. We cannot afford to upset them.' ARGH! I hate that kind of thinking. It ensures that you create magazines and comic books aimed at the tiny percent who write letters of complaint rather than the tens of thousands who don't. Madness. Publishing today. I went back to my office, passing evangelist Lester Sumrall in the corridor. The very sight of him made my mind up and put in a call to Marvel. I started working for them the following month as an editor.

Always make a good impression on your first day. My plan was to be first in as soon as the doors were opened. Unfortunately I misjudged trains at the slightly busy Clapham Junction and found myself on a non-stop to Kent rather than the four-minute trip to Waterloo. I wasn't the first in when I finally turned up at Arundel House at 10:45am. Thankfully, Marvel UK's time code was a little different to the *Saturday Evening Post Magazine* where I'd actually had to punch the clock each day. At Marvel you came in and just got the job done. Time went out the window. The office was in a fab location on the bank of the River Thames at Temple, a part of the city of London that had been established by the Knights Templar back in the Crusades. The chimney pots atop Arundel House dated from Tudor times. I would find myself up among them on many an occasion.

Marvel Comics editor and fan. Unsure which is which.

First up though was Spider-Man's 30th Anniversary. As I was editing the Spidey comic I thought it was the perfect time to bring in some promotion. However, the media did not agree. At that moment in time they couldn't have cared less whether Spider-Man was 30 or 130. To them it simply wasn't a news story. I would have to think again. In the meantime I found that the location of the London office was very handy for lunch with the Strips Dept of the *Daily Mirror*. Over one such lunch with John M. Burns, strips editor John Allard, and *Perishers* creator Maurice Dodd, I mentioned my new Marvelous job. 'Those idiots,' said John A. 'We've been wanting to run the Spider-Man daily strip for the last six months but their licensing department doesn't bother responding to our phone calls or letters.' I thought there must surely be some mistake as Spidey in the *Mirror* would be a fantastic daily promotion for the company. I promised to look into it on my return from lunch. I found that I was right. There was some mistake. The mistake was called Marvel's Licensing Dept. They held office on the top floor of Arundel House. They had the carpets, view and curtains while we in editorial had the floorboards. 'Oh yes,' said their Glorious Leader who shall remain nameless so I can tell it like it was. 'Leave it with us. We'll get back to them.' They never did so the *Daily Mirror* remained Spiderless. Strike one of 3,567.

My wife Jane, strolling in Chelsea one day, discovered the Jane Asher Cake Shop. She went in and was surprised to be served by former Beatle girlfriend and actress Jane herself with a cuppa and cake. When I heard the tale that night it gave me an idea. Back at Marvel the next morning I phoned through and spoke to Jane asking if she would make a cake to celebrate Spider-Man's 30th anniversary. She thought it sounded fun and agreed at a cost of £185. She also agreed to me bringing Spider-Man himself around to the shop to collect it along with as many newspaper photographers as we could muster. I got back in touch with all the nationals and found that now they were interested. Spidey meets Jane Asher with a cake was a news story and a photo op. I was also able to sell the idea to TV and radio programmes. I ended up with seven TV spots over a two day period. Not a bad promotion for an outgoing of £185. And that would have been the total cost but for the fact that our Licensing Dept got to hear of my plans. They weren't happy. 'This doesn't really fit in with our plans,'

I was told. 'What plans?' I asked. 'Who have you got to play Spider-Man?' they asked, changing the subject. 'I have an actor friend who is fairly pumped up and has agreed to play the part for the two days,' I said. 'Is he American?' 'No, he's Dutch.' Sharp intake of breath. 'Well that won't do. Spider-Man's American!' Sharper intake of breath from me this time. 'I am aware of that. My actor friend is very good at accents.' The Heads of Licensing shook in the negative. 'Leave it with us,' they said ominously. That was the day that the Marvel Editorial Dept started calling the Licensing Dept the *Fucking* Licensing Dept.

The following day all hell broke loose. I was summoned to a meeting of the heads of the Editorial and Licensing Departments. I was informed that New York wasn't happy at all with what I'd done. They were so unhappy that they were sending over two of their top guys from management the very next day to try to 'clean up this mess'. I had to ask: 'What mess?' I was told that promotions of any kind must be handled carefully and only at certain times each year. 'But we have comics out every week of each year,' I protested. 'We need to promote them all the time.' Shaking of heads. 'Your promotions are not in line with the general directive,' declared the Licensing Head, showing her Dalek roots.

Sure enough the two Top Guys arrived a day later. We kicked off with what was the most pointless meeting of my life. A five-hour meeting talking about a cake. They were concerned that Jane's cake might not meet management requirements for images of Spider-Man. 'It's a cake,' I protested. 'Doesn't matter if it's a John Deer tractor. If it's in the image of Spider-Man it must meet our standards. Where are Jane's plans for the cake?' Now I knew for a fact that Jane wouldn't draw detailed plans in her cookery. She would just make the bloody cake. I also knew I was not going to ask her to draw plans for such a cake. And so I said: 'Okay, I'll go and phone her and get her to taxi round the plans.' Once out of the room I hurried down to the Marvel basement where we kept our artists. I explained my predicament. They were happy to help. Twenty minutes later I had my detailed plans for the Spidey cake. I took them back into the meeting room. The Licensing mugs poured over them, humming and harring. 'We will still need to see the cake before we let it go on television,' one of them declared. Purely as a joke I then said, 'Maybe we should get Jane to make a second stand-by cake in case the first one doesn't come up to requirements?' Instead of telling me to fuck off like I expected, the knobs actually said: 'Great idea! Get her on it now.' Out of the room and on the phone to Jane. I explain the situation. She laughs loud and long. 'I've worked for such people before,' she assures me. 'So can you make a second cake for us and please do me a favour and charge the earth because all thoughts of saving the company money have now gone out of the window with them shipping folk over from New York.' Second cake in the oven.

On the next day these knobs auditioned my actor friend to play Spider-Man. We had a rather moth-eaten costume that looked like it had been stuck in a drawer for years. But the costume is such a great design that it immediately comes to life with the right body type inside it. My mate bounded into the office in front of the New Yorkers and our own UK Marketing Dept. Several Spidey-like leaps and dives around the room ended at the window, which was thrown up and, in a single bound, my friend dramatically jumped outside. Keeping in mind that we were on the second floor and this was Bill rather than Peter Parker, it was one hell of an audition. He was even wisecracking as he clung to the ledge outside. After Bill had left, the judgement came down. They thought he had filled the costume adequately but that his accent let him down (rubbish! He had a more believable accent than the New Yorkers), and so we would use Bill merely for the newspaper photos but bring a real live American actor over for the TV spots. Ker-Ching! This cheapo-cheapo promotion was now ringing up big bucks.

The day arrived when the cakes were finished. I accompanied the combined Marketing Departments in a taxi over to Jane Asher's Cake Shop in Chelsea. She had placed both cakes on pedestals on a table top. Jane and I shared a look of amusement as the Marketing folk set off on an exploratory tour round the table, ducking and diving as they went to get the best view of both cakes. Standing back, their leader nodded in satisfaction although he couldn't resist pointing out: 'You've missed a bit of colouring on the bottom edge of the second cake.' Jane assured him that would be dealt with before the press arrival the following morning.

And they turned up in their hoards. It was quite a sight seeing each

'Where's my dope?'

Jane Asher and cake.

photographer from each national attempting to pose our Spider-Man and Jane Asher *and* cake in a new and fun way. 'Look this way! Look that way! Look the other way! Look up! Look down!' My favourite shot was the one where it looks as if Jane is helping Spidey climb up a drainpipe, all the while clutching one of the huge cakes. Thank God for spider-powers! Jane's two young sons had come along to meet Spider-Man and I presented them with a big load of Marvel goodies. Their Dad, the satirical political cartoonist Gerald Scarfe, was also with them. I took the opportunity to ask him if he would do a cover for my Spider-Man comic. As his sons were listening, he could hardly say no. What a coup! What a day! Time to change Spider-Men for the New York version and jump in a cab to head to Sky TV News. On the way I noticed that this Spidey had rolled up his mask and was busy rolling a huge joint. I could picture the headlines: SPIDER-MAN AND EDITOR CAUGHT IN DRUGS HAUL! Having always been a Just Say No kind of guy, I grabbed his stash and lobbed it out the window as we sped through Kentish Town. This made for a pretty pissed Spidey for the rest of the day. In the Sky TV News studio we were interviewed by Kay Burley who seemed as pissed as Spider-Man at having to do a comics related story. 'What do you think of other super characters such as Superman and Batman?' she asked us. Without a pause, Spider-Man leapt up on her desk and replied: 'You've got to wonder about a guy in a cape.' Nice Spider-like answer.

The next morning found US Spidey and me with a cake on our laps on a plane from London to Liverpool for an appearance on ITV's *This Morning* magazine programme hosted by Richard & Judy. New York had sent us special solid silver Spidey badges to present to R & J. We were accompanied on the flight by Ulrika Jonson who was hosting ITV's *Gladiators* show at the time. Spidey took a liking to Ulrika on first sight. 'Man, will you look at that rack!' he declared. By the time we were in the studio Green Room, I found him down on one knee in front of the lovely Ulrika, presenting her with one of the silver Spideys. She wore it on the show. I kept the other one for my wife as both Spider-Man and I took an instant dislike to Richard and Judy.

By the end of this second day we were booked in to deliver both cakes to London's Children's Hospital. Spider-Man was to make an appearance in the Isolation Ward, waving at the patients through a glass

Seemed like a good idea at the time. Marvel promotion with Fred Talbot.

window as he held up the two cakes. Unfortunately he failed to see a child's plastic chair near the window and tripped head first in a very Ditko-like manner. His Spider-sense was operating in fine form though as he managed to catch both cakes before they hit the ground, and the sickly kiddies duly got their serving of Spidey sugar-rush.

Next day at the office I was told that having Gerald Scarfe do a cover for us wasn't on as it would not go down well with the fans. I explained that it would bring us new fans and also be quite a news story but there was no convincing. 'Tell him he can do a feature page inside the comic but not the cover,' suggested my MD. Yeah, right! And so we didn't get the Scarfe cover. It still irks all these years later.

CHAPTER 14

1992–1995
The South Bank Show

Hitting the fifth decade anniversary of Marvel Comics I wrote a letter to Melvyn Bragg, producer of London Weekend Television's *South Bank Show* documentary series suggesting the Marvel tale captured a part of American culture that deserved chronicling. To my surprise I was invited to a meeting directly across the Thames in LWT's tower block. Melvyn invited me to co-produce the episode along with his Senior Director Daniel Wiles. What an opportunity both for Marvel and for me! Yes, please. It was agreed that we would split the programme in half, filming part one in New York while part two would be shot in our London office showing how UK talent was breaking into the super-hero world. Fantastic promotion for Marvel as a whole. Who could possibly have a problem with that? Cue my office phone. It was the Licensing Dept from upstairs. 'What's this we hear about the *South Bank Show* producing an episode about Marvel? We would never have agreed to this. The timing is all wrong. We would have chosen to do something like this two years from now.' I counted ten extremely quickly. 'Well do something like this two years from now as well. We will still be here and still need promotions. The editorial department is putting out material now which means we need to promote it now!' Amazing. Not one swear word left my gob, but there was a dictionary full of them cluttering up my brain.

We went ahead. A wonderful learning curve for me working alongside Daniel Wiles who became a friend for life. We laughed at the same things and same people. Arriving in New York we found a film crew setting up outside our hotel in Times Square. As we were heading in, Arnold Schwarzenegger was coming out to film a promotion for his latest movie. We were there for a week but determined to shoot all necessary footage over three or four days so we could have the rest of the time gadding about the city.

Arriving at Marvel early the following morning, our film crew set up establishing shots of the skyscraper base along with passing yellow cabs. Once inside I was warned by the Head of Marketing not to mention DC Comics at all during our interview with Stan Lee. 'Under no circumstances mention Superman or Batman as we do not want to promote our rival. And I will stop the interview if you do not stick to this rule.' Nice welcome. Stan arrives and tells us we can ask him anything as long as it relates to the last five minutes. 'I can't remember a thing before that,' he laughs. On our first question about how he got into the business, Stan details the creation of DC Comics and the birth of Superman and Batman 'who we owe everything to.' I see the Head of Marketing tense off camera but she knows better than to stop Stan the Man. One of those great interviews as Stan covered comic book ground from the Thirties through to the present.

Back in the UK I had a bright idea for the opening shot of the programme. We would go up on the rooftop of LWT and pan downriver from Waterloo Bridge up the Embankment to the Marvel UK office at Temple where we would have Spider-Man skittering around amongst the chimney pots as a voiceover announced that America's finest comic book company was now taking over Britain. It was a great clip that stands up today alongside Stan's interview. To promote the episode, the *South Bank Show* held a Comic Book Workshop on a boat on the Thames. This turned into a show I developed further to play in schools and art centres both in the UK and US. My brother Jason had joined Marvel as an editor by this time and he did the honours in the Spider-suit on this day.

CHAPTER 15

1993–1994
Head of Special Projects

By this time I had become the Head of Special Projects at Marvel, which suited me as it meant nobody knew what I was working on at any given time. During one editorial meeting I made the suggestion that as Marvel had been a successful part of the Macy's Thanksgiving Day Parade for a number of years we could do a similar event in the UK. For example the Lord Mayor's Parade. The MD liked the idea and said, 'Go do it.' It wasn't long before I regretted making that suggestion.

The first thing you get after handing over your cash to the Lord Mayor's office is a fifty page Book of Rules For Attendance in the Parade. I must get round to reading it one day. I was too busy at the time designing the official Marvel float. Big as a double decker bus, because that's exactly what it was underneath all the explosive illustrations of Marvel's finest. I made sure there was a nice mix of Marvel US and Marvel UK creations. It looked good on paper and even better on the bus! I booked for ten super-hero costumes to be shipped over from our New York office. The idea was to hire American size actors to fill the suits on the day of the parade. However, the float went over budget leaving me with zero cash to go in search of actors. Only one thing to do… head round the Marvel UK offices and convince our editors, writers

The Marvel Comics float in the Lord Mayor's Parade.

The Marvel Comics float in the Lord Mayor's Parade.

Marvel UK editorial staff. Quinn as Doctor Strange.

and illustrators to suit up. For the first time since my Blackpool Circus days I was back in costume, as Doctor Strange, Sorcerer Supreme. He had the warmest cape and as the parade was in November, this was a wise move. It took some convincing to get my British short-arse band of heroes into costume. There was much rolling up of trouser legs and tucking in of tops on the American-sized suits. There was only one thing to do once in costume though and that was to take to the roof-top for a photoshoot. Posing exactly like the characters we'd seen a million times in the comics we looked pretty darn good if I say so my-self. Wolverine in particular put the comic into our group photo.

The night before the parade I received a call from the New York office. 'You won't get the costumes wet, will you? You do realize they come in at a total value of several thousand dollars?' Rain? In Novem-ber in London? Hardly likely, I assured them. So you can imagine my surprise the next morning to wake at 5am to the sound of torrential rain. And it kept up through most of the day. It was also bloody cold. We met at base camp for the parade at 7:30am. My band was in good spirits regardless of the weather. The Lord Mayor's chamberlain came running over to me to say that the designated room we had for suit-ing up had been changed and that we would now have to change in a gentlemen's toilet. 'No we won't!' I blew a gasket as the toilet he suggested was a pit we had already complained about. An argu-ment ensued, which I won by simply shouting the loudest. Brute force from Doctor Strange. Once in costume we headed out to the float in the pouring rain, Captain America using his mighty shield as an um-brella. Standing shivering beside the float for a photo, we were jeered at by a group of passing soldiers who were on the float in front of ours. As if that wasn't bad enough, we were then laughed at by a pass-ing *Blue Peter* presenter. I guess on ground level we did look a pretty weedy bunch. It was a different scene by the time we took our places atop the float. We looked truly Marvelous (it had to be said). Off we trundled. Five bloody hours we were on that float, waving down to the millions of people lining the route across London. It is something I will never forget. The rain, the cold and being cheered round Lon-don's landmarks. An image that comes to mind is of Spider-Man, half-way round the course, rolling his mask up in an attempt to get a bit of warmth from a crafty cigarette.

Finally it was over. One quick change and we carted the sodden costumes back to the editorial office where we turned the heat up to high and draped them around the room. As it was Saturday, we hoped they would be dry by Monday morning. And everything was dry by Monday morning. I shoved all costumes carefully back into the packing crate and had it collected for Return to Sender. We were featured strongly on TV coverage of the parade but it was a lot of work for one day's telly.

'Keep in mind that our audience of readers are fourteen year-old morons.' So declared my immediate boss at Marvel UK. I hadn't been aware of this. I'd never had any desire to do anything for morons of any age. But this was his view and it could be argued if you look at the material we were putting out at this time that this could be the only explanation for the direction the books were taking. I sat in on one editorial meeting where the main thrust was trying to come up with more titles with the word 'Death' in them. I suggested 'Deaf Old Git'. The books we were putting into the US had an initial success but sales dropped drastically from issue two onwards. I guess the fourteen year-old morons of America had better things to spend their money on. This was still a time when the word Marvel on a comic would guarantee readers picking up the first issue at least. But those readers weren't going to hang around if they didn't like what they found on opening each book.

Big Head.

EXTENSION: 67941/63808
DIRECT LINE: 081 576 7941
FAX: 081 576 7624

BRITISH BROADCASTING CORPORATION
TELEVISION CENTRE
WOOD LANE, LONDON W12 7RJ
TELEPHONE: 081-743-8000
TELEX: 265781
CABLES: TELECASTS, LONDON

3 June 1994

Mr Tim Quinn
Head of Special Projects
Marvel Comics Ltd
Arundel House
13/15 Arundel Street
London WC2R 3DX

Dear Tim,

Sorry not to have got back to you before, regarding your letter of 9 March.

I am keen to explore the possible television application of the Marvel Comic characters.

However, at present your outline poses two questions for me:

1. What is the look and feel, ie. how do we do justice to the flight of imagination which the two-dimensional comics allow, if we physicalise them? (This would obviously be less of a problem with a feature film type budget).

2. How do we avoid comparisons with Gladiators?
    (I am not keen to try and emulate their formula, but am eager to compete for their audience).

I am very happy to meet and discuss this further, as and when you may with to do so.

Yours sincerely,

MICHAEL LEGGO
Head of Light Entertainment

PRINTED ON RECYCLED PAPER

Bright ideas.

CHAPTER 16

1994

Enid Blyton

At the next editorial meeting our MD asked for ideas outside the super-hero line. I suggested producing a weekly title adapting the work of Enid Blyton into the comic strip format. Blyton's books had sold well since the twenties so grandparents, parents and children themselves were a guaranteed audience. Various editors round the table objected.

'Blyton's racist!'

'She's sexist!'

'Enid Blyton is a fascist!'

Luckily our MD shared all of these personality traits and told me to look into the idea. Blyton, of course, was none of these things, but our idiot PC world of the media had been taking snipes at her success for years. For me the important thing was that children loved her stories and were hooked by the end of the first paragraph.

I set up a meeting with Enid's elder daughter, Gillian Baverstock. Gillian had successfully run the Enid Blyton Company since her mother's death years before. She was everything you would want the head of such a company to be. We hit it off right away and set about choosing the best stories to make up a weekly comic. I wanted to use Marvel style artists to bring Blyton's stories to exciting life. Back at the office I told Sal Buscema, a US illustrator over on his holidays, about the comic. He hadn't heard of Enid Blyton so I quickly gave him a rundown of one of her books, *The Wishing Chair*. Every so often the Wishing Chair would grow wings on each leg and whisk two children and their pixie friend off for adventure after adventure in places such as the Land of Giants, the Land of Fairy Tales, or the Land of Stupids. As I spoke he picked up a pencil and produced a wonderful sketch of two kids holding on for dear life as a winged chair soared over the rooftops of a town. Yes, this was going to work!

From the sublime to the ridiculous. I got a call from Paul Raymond no less. He knew I was writing the *Jane* strip in the *Daily Mirror* and thought it would be a good idea to have a double-page naughty-but-nice strip in his monthly publication *Club International*. I thought so too when he told me the fee. I nipped down into the Marvel basement and asked the assembled artists if anyone fancied illustrating such a strip. All hands went up and that's pretty much how the strip was done from thereon. I would hand in the script down in the basement and everybody would pitch in to the glorious adventures of *SEXBOMB*, a Marvel type heroine whose superpower was that she could give anyone an instant orgasm thereby stopping them in their tracks. Subtle or what? We just had to make sure the strip was out of sight whenever we allowed any children in to tour the Marvel offices. The strip ran for about a year and surely to goodness should be at the top of any Marvel UK fan's Collect List!

Celebrating Enid's centenary.

CHAPTER 17

1993–1994
Beatles, Fairy Tales and Idjuts

Meanwhile back in the US I was also working on the Marvel Music line of books. This was the very simple idea of getting top musicians to work with our illustrators and writers to create something a little different. Alice Cooper was first up working alongside Neil Gaiman. Arriving at Marvel one day Alice's first words to me were, 'Hey, man, where's the john?' I treasure those words as much as the book and album he produced for Marvel. Different, quirky, wonderful. The Rolling Stones, Bernie Taupin and Elton John and the Beatles were next. I contacted Derek Taylor, publicist at the Beatles' Apple company, and arranged a meeting with Neil Aspinall, the Fabs' manager of sorts. Neil had been with them from the start and knew them through and through. He asked me who was going to dialogue this retelling of the Beatles story. I told him that I was putting myself up for that position. 'But how will you have them talking?' This didn't phase me and I answered, 'Well I know how they talk. I've seen *A Hard Day's Night* and *Help!* many times.' Neil shook his head. 'That's not how they talk.' Oh! I admitted defeat. 'In that case we need someone on the inside to write the book,' I said, turning to Derek. 'How about it?' Derek was happy to work for Marvel on creating the comic book tale of the Beatles as he had never written a strip before. 'I'll guide you,' I promised. And so for the whole of that summer Derek and I would meet over lunch every Friday to discuss the project. The lunch would last through dinner time and I swear we always spent a good five minutes talking about the Beatles project. The rest of the time was spent listening to Derek's amazing tales of his life in music. That suited me.

Just another day at Marvel Comics.

Christmas fell at the end of this particular year, just like most years. I had the bright idea of releasing a Father Christmas comic in mid-November to get children in the yuletide spirit. The book would feature a strip story about FC along with puzzles and festive features. Scripts were written and all was go until I was called into an editorial meeting where our Head of Marketing declared: 'We shouldn't risk launching a comic with a new character at this time.' I explained that this was hardly a new character but there was no moving the thick get. Voices were raised and doors were slammed but the book remained canned.

Still in Fairy Tale mode, I put together the dummy first issue of *Happily Ever After?*, a series of sequels to the world's most famous fairy tales. It had never seemed right to me that such wonderful characters as Snow White, Jack of the Beanstalk, Cinderella, Aladdin, Sleeping Beauty, *etc.*, had only ever had one adventure and then settled

That brand new character Father Christmas.
Rough for proposed Christmas comic for Marvel.

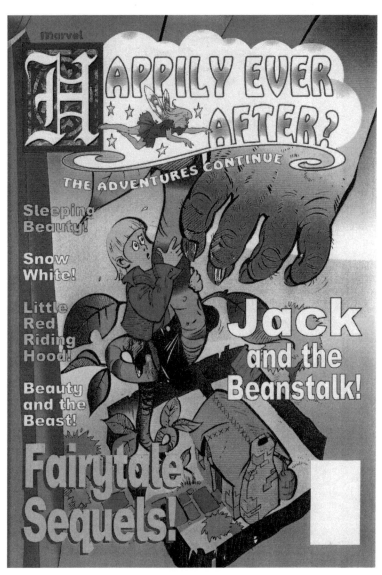

Marvel fairy tale sequels dummy cover.

for living happily ever after. This comic book would take up the tale two weeks after the end of their original adventures. Each tale in the comic would feature a completely different art style. I wanted to reclaim these characters from the Disney look and bring them back to their European roots. As the pages came in, the project looked better with each day.

And then Marvel Comics went bankrupt.

Yes, the top selling comic book company in the world went bankrupt.

Suddenly there was no money anywhere. Every upcoming project was canned. People were fired or 'let go'. So many people were let go one Black Friday that by the time Monday came around management realised we no longer had enough people in house to do the work we were still producing, so a phone call was made to bring back somebody who had been fired three days earlier. Definition of management: Goldbrickin' meatheads.

So there I was one fine day, sitting at my desk, packing up artwork to send back to one of our artists. In came the MD. He noticed I was using a hard-backed envelope. 'Do you know how much those things cost?' he asked. 'And they add to the cost of the postage too. Use a normal envelope.' We were watching costs by this time, you see. The Accounts Manager had overheard this conversation. She came over to me and revealed that our glorious heffalump of a boss had just handed her a £500 receipt for his lunch at the Savoy that day. This was pretty common practice as it turned out. Teaming up with another member of staff we realised that the company would soon go belly-up under this guy's management, not just because of his lunches but also his general lack of savvy about the business. We decided there and then to put together a dossier on the bloater to send over to New York to get them to either kick his ass into gear or out of the company. Over a period of six months the dossier became almost as fat as the man it was about. We shipped it Special Delivery. Next thing we knew, a delegation of Marvel Management arrived at the offices in London early one morning. By midday we had a brand new MD. There was a good feeling at the Edgar Wallace pub that night. We would survive.

Ha!

CHAPTER 18

1994-1995
Radio Ga-Ga

And then I got a call from BBC Radio 1. I had completely forgotten that twelve months previously I had sent their programme controller the suggestion of creating a daily cliffhanger drama series featuring Spider-Man and assorted Marvel characters. He now invited me in to talk the project through. A successful meeting led to me being introduced to Dirk Maggs, producer extraordinary. We got on from the get go and had soon knocked up the overall storyline for a fifty-episode serial of five minute segments. Our aim was to recapture the sheer joy of Stan Lee's Marvel Universe stories from the sixties. Dirk pulled in a masterly group of actors, and one of the highlights of my career was watching him conduct them like an orchestra in the studio. The end result was the most visual comic book I have ever worked on despite there being no illustrations created. The music helped. I'd written to Brian May of Queen to see if he had any interest in composing a Spider-Man theme. To my surprise, he did. I turned up for a meeting at his office and suddenly caught sight of myself in the reflection of the glass door as I entered the building. I was wearing jeans, a white shirt and black waistcoat. This was a look I'd worn for years but suddenly had the awful realisation that with the mop top of curly hair I appeared to be a tribute act to Brian. Meeting me in the foyer, Brian did

Dirk Maggs and Tim Quinn performing their ABBA tribute.

Tim Quinn
Marvel Comics Ltd
Arundel House
13-15 Arundel Street
London WC2R 3DX

11 February 1993

Dear Tim,

Thanks for the great books, which I am perusing avidly. It is
a very inspiring thought, and I have a feeling that it may be
a great collaboration. Anyone with a letter head like yours _must_
be worth talking to !

Cheers,

lib's both . . . . !

Brian May

He's right.

105

'Have we met before?' Brian May atop BBC Broadcasting House.

a double-take. 'Have we met before?' 'Maybe in the bathroom mirror earlier today,' I answered. Despite this, we got on very well, which may have something to do with the Marvel goody bag I presented him with. I was invited down to his home studio the following week. His house was typical rock star domain. Suits of armour stood between pinball machines. Entering the studio, Brian handed me THE guitar and suggested I play. Unworthy doesn't come close. He flipped a few levers and dials and his brand new Spider-Man theme blasted out of the speakers. It was and is like nothing I have ever heard before or since. Amazing Spider-Man. As Brian's guitar let rip, images of Spidey skittering around the walls and ceiling of the studio came to mind.

And so we came to launch day for the radio series. It had already garnered more media interest and press attention than anything else created by Marvel UK. I was about to head out to the launch event when, passing through the Marvel foyer I was stopped by The Boss. 'Why are we bothering with this radio nonsense?' he asked. Now this radio nonsense had taken a lot of work outside office hours from myself. Also, it was a brilliant idea. So I was a little put out by the moronic question and answered slowly so that even an amoeba would get my drift: 'To… promote… our… product… so… people… buy… it.' Our attractive young receptionist couldn't resist laughing out loud at this. My boss gave me the 'I'll kill you, you bastard' look beloved of all Victorian mill owners.

The launch was a blast, again attracting a lot of media interest. The first episode of the drama was played to great effect. Back at the office, I found an envelope waiting on my desk. It was my first Letter of Warning. Now you don't want to get a Letter of Warning no matter where you work, but for some reason I could not take this one seriously. For one thing, it had Spider-Man and the Incredible Hulk rampaging across the top of the letterhead. I pinned it up on the main office wall so all my fellow Marvelites could see. The Boss spotted it, pulled it down and banged it back on my desk warning: 'Take it seriously!' 'I can't!' I replied. 'I'm going for the three!' (three Letters of Warning and you are out).

Later that week, my boss entered my office and closed the door behind him. He shook his head as he looked at me.

'You know your problem, Tim?'

'No, can't say I do. Pray tell.'

'You don't know the meaning of the word hierarchy.'

'You're right. I come from Liverpool where we pride ourselves on not knowing the meaning of that word. If I wanted to understand it I would be working for a non-creative company rather than Marvel Comics.'

Hmm. The writing was obviously on the wall.

And then I got a call from Andrew Lloyd-Webber's office. They wanted to see me about an idea I had mailed to them months before. So a few days later I found myself sitting opposite Andrew at his London office. My idea was simple. A musical featuring Marvel comic book characters. Andrew had already taken the unlikely character of the Phantom of the Opera and turned him into a world-wide musical success. He told me that the Marvel idea appealed to him as he saw the romance in normal people being turned into super-heroes, donning skintights, masks and capes and attempting to keep the secret from their girl or boy friend. Andrew asked which of our characters I thought would work best on stage. I told him that some would prove to be impossible to work with such as the Human Torch due to theatre health and safety fire restrictions and Submariner due to the impossibility of showing the undersea world on stage. He stopped me before I could go any further. 'Neither of those would be a problem for us. We can do anything on stage.' Well I liked the sound of that. Andrew suggested I compile a list of which heroes weren't bound to movie or TV deals and come back with my boss in a week's time to push the idea onwards. Sounded good to me. I headed back to the office and told my boss the exciting news. He merely nodded and put it down in his diary. I told him to get the information from New York as to just which characters we would be able to hand over to ALW.

Cut ahead one week. Back in Andrew's office. I introduce my boss. Pleasantries. Tea poured. Andrew: 'So which of your characters can I use?' I turn to my boss. 'Ahh, I haven't found out yet,' he replies. SILENCE as Andrew digests this, his face getting redder as he does so. 'Then why are we having this meeting? Call me when you have the details.' And up and out of the office goes Andrew. As we leave the building my boss turns to me with a heavy sigh and says, 'Do you have any idea how much work this will involve?'

Arundel House, 13/15 Arundel Street, London WC2R 3DX.
Telephone: 071-497 2121. Fax: 071-497 2234.

MEMORANDUM

FROM: ▋▋▋▋▋▋
TO: TIM QUINN

CC: MIKE HOBSON
       CAROLINE AUBREY

DATE: 13 JANUARY 1995

Please take this as your first warning. Three such warnings will result in dismissal. I'm sure I don't need to tell you that continuation of your behaviour at noon today in the front hall can have only one outcome.

Reg. Office: 100 Chalk Farm Road, London NW1. Reg. No. 1034742 VAT No. GB 2335088-74

You will be exterminated!

Time to move on… But first, I had wanted to produce a humour magazine for some time at Marvel, but I didn't want it to end up looking and reading like the countless *Viz* rip-offs. There was a TV series called *The Comic Strip Presents…* that seemed an ideal match. The producer, writer and main actor of the series was a chap by the name of Peter Richardson. Peter liked the idea of collaborating with Marvel especially as he had a brand new series about to launch on the BBC. He asked me to accompany him on a trip to talk with the management at BBC TV Centre. He wanted to show them that Marvel Comics was interested in the series. On the way across London Peter kept noticing huge billboards advertising a new series coming up from Robbie Coltrane. 'Why aren't the BBC doing this with my series?' he asked. I could feel his rage grow as we checked in at BBC reception. By the time we were in the meeting and the BBC executives were smiling nicely and pouring tea in their best china, Peter was like a rumbling volcano beside me. And then he blew. It was a real explosion. Months and months of pent up frustration with his bosses spewed out. I could relate to this. He finished by crashing both hands down on the tabletop causing cups, saucers, milk, tea and biscuits to shoot skywards. And then he strode magnificently from the room, slamming the door behind him. I wanted to applaud but there was that slightly embarrassing moment where I looked around at the execs and they looked back at me. Obviously they couldn't speak while I was still there and so I nodded farewell and went in search of Peter.

He was in a better mood during the few script sessions we had together with his cast, which included the model and author Sara Stockbridge. The magazine was an interesting project but I didn't stay to see it through. Back at Marvel I had had a call from a publisher called Richard Desmond. He was thinking about starting up a comic book department within his company and wondered whether I wanted to head it up. As I was feeling about Marvel much the same way Peter Richardson was feeling about the BBC, and also because my salary would immediately be tripled, I accepted the job. Peter's series, *Glam Metal Detectives*, came out and was barely noticed thanks to the BBC's crafty scheduling and lack of promotion. Marvel put out a *Glam Metal Detectives* mag that looked and read just like all the other *Viz* rip-offs.

The BBC's best kept secret.

CHAPTER 19

1995
Ugh!

And so on to Richard Desmond's company out at Docklands. Richard, or Dirty Des as *Private Eye* have branded him, had recently launched *OK* magazine and wanted to show he was a family publisher to get away from the image created by his top-shelf publications. We were to launch three titles. *Power Rangers*, *Action Man*, and *Sindy*. My first day in the job and I knew I'd made a mistake. Not so much in leaving Marvel as in signing on with RD. I've now sat here for half an hour attempting to think of things I can write about that company and that man that won't see me in court. I was there three months. I ended up being escorted from the building by a security man. I loathed every minute and my flesh crawls at the memories. And so I draw a veil over those three months of my life out at Docklands…

CHAPTER 20

1995–1999
Melvyn Bragg

…And head off to Nashville. I'd kept in with my friends over at LWT's *South Bank Show* and pitched the idea of making a documentary on women in Country Music. At this moment in time a lot of excellent female singer/songwriters were coming out of Nashville. I thought it would be interesting to find out just how they coped in what was predominantly a redneck scene. So, film crew in hand, I jumped aboard one of the first direct flights to Nashville to meet and interview the names of the day. Mary Chapin Carpenter, Kathy Mattea, Pam Tillis, Suzy Bogguss, and the rest. The trip coincided with that year's televised Country Music Awards where I found myself in the celebrity-filled audience sitting behind Julia Roberts and her husband Lyle Lovett. As well as the big names, I thought we should try and showcase a new act on the programme. With this in mind I went on the Gerry House Show at a local radio station. I mentioned that if any new female singer/songwriters were out there they could meet me at Tootsie's Bar Lounge at 1pm that day and to bring a cassette of their work. Sitting in the bar later on I was disappointed at 1:05pm to find nobody had bothered showing until a woman put her head round a doorway at the back of the room and asked: 'Are you the English guy? There're about a hundred girls waiting for you back here.' And so there were. And every one of them had a cassette tape. And every one of them was good if not better than good. I ended up throwing the tapes in the air and featuring the one I caught. Careers are made on such moves!

Melvyn Bragg was a joy to work for. You would pitch the idea for a show and he would give you an instant yes or no. If yes, you'd work out a budget and timescale for filming and editing the show. In the case of the Nashville show the budget was £80,000. The whole thing was a fairly simple operation. I'd make contact with the various people I wanted in the programme, set up a time to film an interview with each of them, and attempt to build a cohesive story that would run for fifty-or-so minutes. Once the editing process was complete, Melvyn would come down and view the rough edit deep beneath LWT's tower block on the banks of the Thames. He would scribble notes as he watched, tearing the pages from his book to hand to me at the end. They were always simple but very effective changes to pull the edit together. That was it. My kind of boss.

Nashville Skyline with Pam Tillis and fellow South Bank Show *producer Daniel Wiles.*

CHAPTER 21

1997
Enid Blyton's Mystery & Suspense

Back in the UK, Enid Blyton was about to celebrate her 100th birthday. At least she would have been had she still been alive. Regardless of this small matter, the publisher Egmont Fleetway decided to launch a brand new Enid Blyton weekly. Enid's elder daughter, Gillian, suggested me for the job of editor. Although we had never got round to publishing the Enid Blyton comic at Marvel, Gillian and I had got on very well and shared much the same view about her Mum's amazing work.

So there I am and all is well on day one at Egmont Fleetway. It only started going downhill from day two. The company wanted the magazine to tie in to a new TV series based on Blyton's *Famous Five* stories. Fair enough. Good idea even, except that they wanted the rest of the magazine to be made up of Enid's other kids-go-after-crooks tales. This was guaranteed to make the magazine a little samey from page to page. I would much rather have featured a variety of Blyton's tales from Fairy Tale type stories to nature, school, Robin Hood and dog exploits. Oh well, I attempted to make sure the illustrators for each story would be completely different from one other, which would give some variety. Egmont had already come up with the name *Enid Blyton's Mystery & Suspense*. With this in mind, I commissioned a dark and brooding cover for issue number one showing the Famous Five in dire straits in a rowing boat on a stormy ocean as an old fashioned galleon is hurled up from the depths and lit by a flash of lightning. Mario Capaldi turned in a stupendous piece of art, which everybody in the office was blown away by. You actually got drenched if you stood too near the painting. Two days later, the picture was pulled as being too dark and gloomy to be the cover of a first issue. 'We want something bright and fun,' I was told. 'But the title is *Mystery & Suspense*,' I argued. 'Surely that means dark and spooky?' Apparently not.

Now my wife Jane had told me to make sure I just nod during editorial meetings from now on, and take the cheque at the end of the month. That had been my intent on arriving at Egmont. But… sitting in an early editorial meeting I was told by the Head of Marketing that she had just been in conversation with the Marketing Dept at Sainsburys. They had told her that they had put a yellow stripe down the edge of their generic brand of All Bran and it had caused a huge increase in sales. 'So I suggest you put a yellow stripe down the edge of the comic, Tim.' I nodded. To be honest, it was all I could do as I was without speech. The HoM did a double-take at me. 'What's up?' 'What do you mean?' I asked. 'That look on your face,' she answered. Betrayed by my own face. It was at that moment I realised I was in a place Enid Blyton had created many years previously. She called it The Land of Stupids.

I'd been promised that Egmont would be putting on a huge promotion for the launch. One month from D Day I raised the subject again. I was told that the plan had been changed. We were going to launch the magazine with zero promotion and wait six months until we knew who our readership was so that we could then aim our promotions directly at that group. 'But we already know that a large percentage of our audience will be Enid Blyton readers,' I protested. 'Shouldn't we let them know?' Nope. We would wait six months. Sound stupid to you? Me too.

Speaking of the launch, I suggested organising a launch party. For some unknown reason this was agreed to but I was told to only invite important people to the party. 'Yeah, our contributors,' I said. 'No, not them,' explained my Group Leader. 'Just the printers and marketing department.' That day I mailed out invitations to every illustrator and writer I had ever worked with.

One of these was Jemima Rooper. She was a fourteen year-old actress who was playing the part of George the tomboy in the ITV *Famous Five* series. I'd already interviewed her and asked her to adapt one of Blyton's stories for the mag. She turned in a superb adaptation that captured the visual elements of the story perfectly. Jemima was a very natural writer. She agreed to write regularly for the magazine. When I told my Group Leader back at Egmont he asked her age. 'Fourteen? Great we can give her a child's rate.' Bloody typical. There are so few good writers in comic books and here was one we should have been encouraging. Not that it really mattered as Jemima has gone on to a golden career, starring on TV, in the West End and on Broadway. Child's rate! Idiot!

Enid Blyton's Famous Five *and Timmy the Editor.*

And it gets worse. Another management bozo at Egmont suggested I make one of the Famous Five black. 'No problem,' I said. 'But we shall have to make them all black as they are all from the same family.' This wouldn't do, of course, so the Famous Five remained as Blyton had created them forty years earlier.

The launch was fun. Denis Gifford, comics historian and writer and illustrator, turned up and deemed the mag the best children's periodical he had seen in over a decade. He was right, in my modest opinion. The magazine featured the talents of Phil Gascoine, Mario Capaldi, Maureen & Gordon Gray, John Lupton, and Steve Parkhouse. TV's *Famous Five* turned up that night too, and I seem to remember that either Dick or Julian became a little inebriated by the end of the party. Obviously overdoing the lashings of Ginger Beer.

The magazine came out and the cunning plan of Egmont worked. Nobody was aware it was there. Bewilderingly, a member of staff confided in me that it was really important for two high ups at Egmont that the mag should fail as they had launched a magazine the previous year that had flopped and it would look bad for them if this one soared. As I've found way too many times in management, you couldn't make it up. By issue seven, I was called into the Marketing Director's office to be told I was going to be let go.

'Are you canning the mag?' I asked.

'No, it shall keep on running.'

'Will you be changing it?'

'No. Everybody loves what you have done with it.'

'Then why are you firing me?'

'Because we have to be seen to be doing something in light of the poor sales.'

I kid you not. Those were the exact words because I wrote them down immediately after, knowing I wouldn't believe it a day later. Foolishly they gave me the option of going that moment or one week later so that I could hand the mag over to the new editor. I chose to stay on as I had a plan. The following day I contacted every contributor I had ever used and told them to supply me with as much Enid Blyton material as they could over the next few days. Soon as it came in I signed each invoice and sent it up to Accounts. By the time I left the company had enough Blyton material to keep them going over the next two years, which was a shame as the mag only lasted another three issues. Oh dear. What a shame. By this time I was wondering what I was doing in the comic book business. It wasn't much fun any more. I remember my Group Editor at Egmont looking over a strip page of art roughs from that master Mario Capaldi and circling forty-two different points on the page for correction. She claimed his body work was all off. It wasn't, but this was another example of somebody needing to be seen to be doing something.

CHAPTER 22

1998–2001
Blue Moon

I was back in the US working for *The Saturday Evening Post Magazine* again as editor on their *US Kids* magazine when I got a fax from Gillian Baverstock. She was Enid Blyton's elder daughter and we had kept in touch since working on the Marvel Blyton dummy. Gillian suggested we team-up and form our own publishing company to put out comic books that would encourage a love of reading in children. Seemed like a great idea to me, so we loaded up the truck and moved to Shrewsbury in Shropshire. The house we chose was massive to serve as both living area and editorial offices. The staircase in the house was from the 1500s so would have matched the Marvel UK chimney pots.

We called the new company Quill Publications, Quill being an amalgam of the name Quinn and Gill. It was decided that our first magazine would be a series of sequels to fairy tales, myths and legends featuring such characters as Jack of the Beanstalk, Puss in Boots, Aladdin, Tom Thumb, Cinderella, Rumpelstiltskin, Medusa, Snow White, Sleeping Beauty, Red Riding Hood, and the Pied Piper. All these characters lived in the same town so they would often bump into each other during their adventures. The whole comic was pulled together by two modern day kids and their dog who could witness these adventures through their Amazing Computer. It turned out that the boy

September 1998   Vol. 11, No. 6

MEET THE FOLKS BEHIND U·S·KIDS

WELCOME!

Hold tight to the pages of this magazine, because it's about to take you on a journey that extends from the rain forests of central Africa to the interior of your own body! Our fantastic puzzles will prove that even math and spelling can be exciting, while the Fairy Tale Sequel and fiction pages show that reading really is fun. There's a step-by-step guide to playing soccer, and our feature on the Tulip Time Scholarship Games is sure to inspire you to get in training for the 1999 event!

Next issue sees the start of a readers' letter page, so write in and let us know the directions you would like to see the magazine traveling in future editions.

Happy reading!

Your friends,
Tim the Editor and Henry the Office Dog

Contents

Visit us on the Web: www.satevepost.org/kidsonline

Cover photo courtesy of American Youth Soccer Organization
Cover illustration by George Sears

Cory SerVaas, M.D.–Editorial Director

Tim Quinn–Editor

Matthew Brinkman–Art Director

Elizabeth O. Terry, R.N. M.S.N., C.P.N.P.–Health/Research Editor

Henry–Office Dog

CORY SERVAAS, M.D.
Editorial Director

TIM QUINN
Editor

MATTHEW BRINKMAN
Art Director

DANIEL LEE
Associate Editor

ELIZABETH O. TERRY, R.N., M.S.N., C.P.N.P.
Health/Research Editor

JACK GRAMLING
Copy Editor

PAT PERRY
Consulting Editor

NANCY TAFFE
Editorial Assistant

ELIZABETH PETERSON, M.D.
C. WILLIAM HANKE, M.D. FACP
WILLIAM H. BEESON, M.D.
Medical Consultants

GREG JORAY
Executive Publisher

ERIC SERVAAS
Associate Publisher

SUSAN HANLEY
Circulation Manager

DWIGHT LAMB
Production Director

MIKE BIRGE
Production Manager

PATRICIA A. STRICKER
Compositor

TONY REITZ
TERESA HROMADA
Interns

One of the children's magazines at The Saturday Evening Post Magazine.

was actually the once and future king Arthur. I brought in a variety of illustrators from Marvel Comics and other places I'd worked both in the UK and the US. Gillian, Jane and I wrote the stories. We also included beautifully illustrated poetry and history pages. The idea was to plant seeds of interest in a variety of subjects in our readers.

The whole thing came together over a six-month period and looked great. This was definitely a project that could develop in any number of interesting ways. We brought in a distribution company who promised they would get us into every possible outlet across the UK. BBC Radio 4 created a programme to follow us from initial idea to launch and beyond. The media caught on and were keen to promote the idea of a guy from Marvel teaming up with the daughter of Enid Blyton. Gillian's writing was great, certainly in line with her Mum's. We came up with the name *Blue Moon* for the comic. This was the name of the land where the characters lived.

The week leading up to the launch had stories in most of the national newspapers. On launch day the BBC Radio 4 programme suggested they record Gillian and I as we headed into the Sloane Square WH Smiths to pick up our copy of the published comic. Great idea. Except. It. Wasn't. There. Microphone in our faces as we were asked how this made us feel. Phone call to our distributor who asks: 'Are you sure it's not there? It should be.' We were sure. It wasn't there. Nor was it there the next day or the day after that. It finally arrived four days late thanks to the skill of our distribution company. This made all our promotions pointless. Customers might go back on the second day. Maybe even the third, but no way would they still be looking on day four. And it was the same problem up and down the country. Similar story with the following issue. Two days late. And issue three. The distributor assured us each time that this problem would be sorted but it never was. However, the readers who were picking up the comic loved it. We started getting letters from teachers who were using it during Literacy Hour. Parents, grandparents and, most important of all, children themselves loved the stories. The letters were very heartening. But the sales simply didn't pick up enough after the fiasco of the launch issue.

We got an email from Stan Lee who had seen the first three issues. He liked them and told us about the new website he had just launched and that there might be room for a possible link-up to *Blue Moon*. Well that was exciting. Not quite as exciting as when Stan's website went bust a very short time later, but still exciting. The comic looked better with each edition, and so we plodded on from issue to issue, lifted up by letters from readers and brought down by sales figures. It simply wasn't catching on fast enough. Thirty-six brand new pages every issue cost a lot to produce. Slowly but surely we were sinking. After issue twelve we sunk. It was a tough week. On the Monday Jane's mother died. On the Tuesday our company went belly-up and we lost everything including our house. I spoke with my Dad on the phone that night and he gave me the Dad advice: 'Never mind, son. You've got your health.' Unfortunately, the following day Jane was diagnosed with a brain tumour. This was really turning out to be a very bad week indeed.

Enid Blyton's elder daughter Gillian Baverstock, her dog Bruce and TQ at the Blue Moon *office door.*

Blue Moon 6

Blue Moon 8

CHAPTER 23

2002–2016

"Life is what happens while you are busy making other plans."

What can I tell you after that? Everything changed. Everything. As John Lennon once said, life is what happens while you are busy making other plans. To prove his point he then went and got himself shot. Nothing quite so drastic here. For the next two years we lived in a garden shed. Honest. Admittedly the garden shed was in a millionaire belt outside London and our neighbours were rock and pop stars from the sixties, but it was still a bloody garden shed. Jane went through various hellish depleting operations, the after effects, which still shudder through to this day. I suspect we both went a bit nuts because in the midst of all this we formed our own management company and started working with musicians and bands putting on tours, concerts and charity shows. An interesting bunch of characters they were too with Billy Wyman, Donovan, Albert Lee, John Paul Jones, Kiki Dee, Julie Felix, Steve Harley & Cockney Rebel to name but a few crossing our musical path. Happily we were no longer living in a garden shed but rather back where I once belonged in Merseyside. All roads lead to Home.

And Merseyside now has its own television station, Bay TV

Liverpool. Sitting over a cuppa or two with good friend and musician of musicians Craig LW, we got talking about our love of the Mersey Beat period from the early sixties. On the spot we determined to set off and interview many of the surviving 'groups' from that time. On a whim we strolled over to Bay TV and sold them the idea on the spot. So for the last few months we have had the delightful job of interviewing our heroes in front of the telly cameras capturing amazing tales from that most heady of decades. Total joy to be compiling these stories and editing them into a series of documentaries. We are also filming complete concerts featuring these artists down in Liverpool's legendary Cavern Club. They can still blast it out, fifty years on! At heart, I'd always wanted to be a Beatle but missed the boat when they were hiring, so this is as close as I'm likely to get.

And speaking of history, one of the highlights of 2015 was being contacted by Miwk Publishing who wanted to gather together the *Doctor Who* strips produced by Dicky Howett and myself back in the dawn of time. I don't think that either of us had been aware of how many of these strips we had done. And some of them were actually funny! The first print run has just sold out. Shocked and stunned doesn't come close. It's only taken me 45 years to find a publisher who knows what they are doing. You've got to laugh.

Proud father.

I do keep a hand in magazines these days. About ten years ago I realised that there were no longer any magazines on the newsstands that I bought each month. This came as a shock because along with comic books I had always loved various magazines for their style and personality. Suddenly there was no periodical I couldn't wait to come out each month. The newsstands looked dull and stupid with covers blazing the delights of *X-Factor* or other trash programmes. Gillian Baverstock suggested I rectify this by heading into schools and finding the next generation of journalists. She had noticed that very few schools had school magazines these days. That seemed nuts as these gave opportunities for non-academic students to shine in their own way.

Trying to sell a book to the Impossible Girl.

So during the last decade I have been going into schools across the UK and working with editorial teams of students to produce brand new general interest magazines. The intent is that they will look and read as good as anything on the newsstands (that's not difficult). My aim is to be able to take a copy of these magazines and hand it to someone in New York or Sydney and for them to immediately want to know when the next edition is coming out. I'm very proud of the work of my students. The magazines shine out in comparison to the tripe put out by professional publishers, and it is the work of kids. They put their heart, soul and humour into these magazines and there is the difference. Many famous names have helped support this venture by allowing me to take groups of students to interview them. All of these names have been blown away by the resulting magazine. Sir Tim Rice, Jeffrey Archer, Jeremy Paxman, Melvyn Bragg, Willy Russell, Helen Skelton, David Morrissey, Bill Wyman, Deborah Meaden, Julian Clary, and the list goes on… Are there comic strips in these magazines? But of course! The story continues…

Quinn & Howett in the Coal Hill Retirement Home.

Sal Buscema cover rough.

Seemed like a good idea at the time. Marvel promotion.

Tim Quinn is pictured with comic superhero Spider-Man.

With great power comes great responsibility. Editor and edited.

In my spare time I like to fight crime. Mighty Quinn and Boy Wonder.

With Katy Manning.

With Katy.

X-Man.

School mag Quinn style.

DRAWING BREATH

DICKY HOWETT

I remember exactly where I was the moment I heard that President Kennedy had been assassinated. I also remember exactly where I was the moment I saw Dicky's artwork for the first time. Coincidence? I think not. My reaction that day was a mighty 'What on earth is that?' (to Dicky's artwork, not Kennedy's demise), but I soon cracked the code and have been laughing at him ever since (Dicky not Kennedy). On that long ago day, Dicky's work did not blend in beside the art of his fellow cartoonists at IPC, DC Thomson, Marvel Comics, or even *Club International*. His style stood out like a clown in a church pulpit. It jarred, and I loved it.

As I type these words, it is print week for this jarring book. I have in front of me the very latest Quinn & Howett page of funnies that will see print in the 500th edition of *Doctor Who Magazine*. Bloody fine script but the artwork has me LOLing out loud. (For Comic Book Completists: 45 years of scripts available from Mighty Quinn Management. Look great framed. Perfect Christmas gift).

Reading Dicky's story for the first time caused me much astonishment as I had always assumed that when we weren't working together he was just sat in a chair, smoking a pipe, waiting for my call. I never knew he had so much in him. It was/is a thoroughly enjoyable partnership, and I think we both deserve the *Fictional Best Cartoon Team of the Year* Award.

– Tim Quinn & **www.mightyquinnmanagement.com**

ISBN 978-1-908630-63-6

Biography

£15.99 RRP

Cover design **Andrew Orton**

Also available:

with Tim Quinn
It's Even Bigger on the Inside

by Tim Quinn
Argh!

DRAWING
BREATH

DICKY HOWETT

Drawing Breath

Second paperback edition published September 2016 by
Miwk Publishing Ltd, 45A Bell St, Reigate, RH2 7AQ.

ISBN 978-1-908630-63-6

A CIP catalogue record for this book is available from the British Library.

Design by Andrew Orton.
Typeset in Sabon and Trade Gothic.

Printed and bound by TJ International, Cornwall.

www.miwkpublishing.com
This product was lovingly Miwk made.

For Lily, Poppy, Toby, Teasel and Nell. What Grampy did!

CHAPTER 1

The Rough Draft Years

Adolf Hitler entered my life with a real bang. Early in 1945, he lobbed a V2 rocket into our street and like any good comedy act, he brought the house down. Thus from a very early age, humour was ingrained (and after my mum and I were dug from the wreckage) there was absolutely no escaping my fate. To underline the point, a few years later, my Ardleigh Green primary school report provided me with yet *another* rocket which read, 'Would make a good cartoonist'. Evidently I was academically damned, with very faint praise, from that moment on.

At the beginning of the 1950s, the *Eagle* comic loomed large with *Dan Dare Pilot of the Future*, featuring prominently in full colour on the front pages. I ignored the rest of the comic. I was not at all interested in cutaway drawings of internal combustion mechanicals, or the lives of various good guys (on the back pages) or *Riding the Range* (even though written by Charles Chilton of *Jet Morgan* fame). However, I did notice that a certain 'Frank Hampson' drew *Dan Dare*. To be frank, I wanted to be Frank. (It was only years later that I discovered that Hampson's studio staff completed most of the finished artwork, copied in minute detail from Frank's immaculate roughs and visuals). I was an avid follow-

er of Dan's adventures, initially with the exquisite story *Operation Saturn* (I joined the comic in 1953 so there it all starts) and I was immediately immersed in the evil doings of the Treens and the Mekon and Doctor Blasco (an early exposure here, you will notice, to a fictional Doctor – albeit an evil one) plus Space Fleet rockets piloted by a bunch of RAF-type Johnnies, nipping off to Venus at many 'hundreds' of miles an hour and taking approximately a weekend to complete the interplanetary crossing. This, it must be noted, was all performed in the far future of '1996' using little more than a few gallons of upgraded aviation fuel and an electronics box full of thermionic valves. The artwork, of course, was superb.

Dicky in May 1945.

My admiration for Dan and company wavered somewhat when in 1955, the *Junior Express Weekly* hit the stands, presenting me with a new space hero, Jeff Hawke 'Pioneer of Space Travel' (The Sydney Jorden strip was a regular feature in the *Daily Express* from 1955 to 1974). The *Junior Express Weekly* was offering readers an exclusive *Jeff Hawke Crew Membership* and the chance to own a special space 'log book'. I applied for mine and was rewarded by being selected as an 'astral navigator'. Not exactly what I wanted, (what was an 'astral' anyway?) The other choices were Radar and Radio, Rocket Engineer and the best, Space Pilot. My pass book was stamped 'passed A1' which was small comfort. However, I did find time to complete a page requiring a 'description of the holder'. I wrote my name, address (in case I got lost in space) age and weight. For a puny eleven year old I gave my weight as 4st and 9oz. (Perhaps I was thinking of a couple of sacks of spuds at the time?) I still have this log book and, believe it or not, I'm now quite a bit heavier.

Radio was big in the 1950s and none bigger than an epic twenty-week rocket ship saga that attracted twenty million listeners, and me. 'The BBC presents Jet Morgan in *Journey into Space*...!' so intoned the sepulchral voice of David Jacobs at the beginning of one of BBC Radio's most successful series of the 1950s. Conceived written and produced by Charles Chilton, these seminal stories of space-flight and strange goings on in space captured the public imagination. Every Monday evening at 7.30pm, the latest cliff-(or in this case asteroid-)hanger was resolved, only to later plunge the listening millions into yet another week of anxious anticipation. This vastly popular series (David Lean even proposed doing a movie version) emptied pubs and caused factory workers to forsake overtime. The programme was considered a landmark in radio drama. From 1953 through to 1955, the BBC made a trilogy of programmes consecutively entitled, *Journey into Space* (re-recorded in 1958 as *Operation Luna*), *The Red Planet* and *The World in Peril*. Each episode was recorded on tape and the evocative background music, composed and conducted by Van Phillips, was swung off discs in situ. Sound effects likewise, these having been recorded at Battersea Power Station and the National Physical Laboratory

at Kingston. (The ominous 'televiewer' sound was, in fact, naval ASDIC). But it was all myth and magic to me. Jet Morgan and crew landing on the Moon and then being whisked back in time to a prehistoric Earth. Were the pictures better on radio? You bet!

Although a working class and relatively threadbare family we, in our house, had a television set. It was a little nine inch black and white Ecko table model and *The Quatermass Experiment* was on! This was a monumental six-part creeping horror of a serial, broadcast live, direct from the BBC's cramped and very outdated studios at Alexandra Palace. So the story goes, a spaceship crash lands and 'something' emerges from the wreckage. It looks like a man, but is it...? Basic stuff, but back then we had not seen the like, and the TV nation sat transfixed. I recall now only one scene. This was from episode five and the camera tracked back to reveal a park bench with a couple sitting on it, chatting away. As the couple leave, the camera pans down and we see 'something' rustling in the bushes behind them. Wooo-hooo.

I watched nearly all the episodes but missed the final part due to my mother failing to wake me in time (I had to pretend to go to bed as my younger brother wasn't allowed to watch 'horror films'). There was no chance of seeing again the bulk of this TV production as only the first two parts were preserved as tele-recordings. But back then telly was supposed to be live and in any case, tele-recording (a linked 35mm film camera looking at a monitor screen) was expensive. Generally, the unions and the cinema industry were sniffy about any form of television 'copying', especially drama.

In June 1953 the very biggest live telly event of the decade was the coronation broadcast. For this, the BBC deployed all of its latest camera equipment with the crews required to wear lounge suits and ties. In one instance, a cameraman was bedecked in full evening dress. During the run up to the coronation date, the nation frantically acquired television sets, and those that didn't, insinuated themselves towards neighbours who had. When June 6th arrived did we invite all our neighbours and friends in to watch the proceedings on our little Ecko? Not a bit of it. Inexplicably, me and my family totally avoided the 'great day' and went on a trip to Southend-on-Sea. We got very wet.

But I hadn't neglected my Destiny. Much time was spent after school in the privacy of my own bedroom, drawing *Superman* strips, little quarter-page four-frame efforts with my own glowing text strap lines on the title page, '*He could out-race a speeding rocket*' – picture of Supie speeding past a rocket. '*His strength knows no limit*' – Supie lifts a block of flats, and '*He can squeeze water from a stone*'. A bit unlikely perhaps, but I recall that in one of the movies, Superman squeezed a fully-cut diamond from a mere lump of coal so I suppose anything is possible. Fifteen years later I went on a frenzied *Superman* comic-buying spree, raiding newsagents for any copies available, this to the infinite bemusement of my wife.

Another definite 1950s cartoon favourite of mine was *Garth*. A *Daily Mirror* newspaper strip, Garth was an all-British mighty man with mythical overtones.

Stephen Dowling and John Allard.

Jumping ahead a bit to 1965, I had the pleasure of meeting *Garth*'s creator Steve Dowling and assistant John Allard, (and later, pre-eminent *Garth* script writer Peter O'Donnell). This was for an article I was considering writing for my amateur science fiction fanzine *Spot Wobble* (more of this later). And so it was with unbelievable ease that I sauntered into the *Mirror* offices (long-since

Supie

demolished) in High Holborn. During our chat, puffing on his pipe, Steve Dowling sketched before my very eyes, a panel for the following week's *Garth* adventure. Effortless skill. When Steve retired, the strip was taken over and drawn by, among others, Frank Bellamy. Not, I fear Frank's finest achievement. His signature 'cinematic' style of artwork gradually coarsened the tone of the strip. Also, Frank had difficulty drawing the nude female form convincingly – '*blokes with tits*' was one pointed comment – and the strip lost much subtlety in the process. A case of 'dumbing down' before the epithet became synonymous. In my eyes *Garth* never really recovered when its originators departed.

Recently I was contacted by a video producer working on a *Garth* documentary. He asked me about the possibility of using the photographs I had taken during my Dowling interview. It now appears that these pictures (just three) are the only existing record of Steve Dowling at work on the *Garth* strip. A piece of cartoon history fortuitously preserved. Chuffed or what?

Although my youthful cartooning attempts kept me off the streets, television encroached again. This occurred one bank holiday during a visit to Southend-on-Sea. Strolling along the prom, I encountered an actual outside broadcast taking place. Television in the 1950s was all-live, and being all-live it needed regular injections of action and adventure. Outside broadcasting provided some ready-made thrills and, in those years, a favourite thrilling venue for both BBC and ITV was Southend-on-Sea. Never a year seemed to go by without Southend Pier (longest in the world at 1¼ miles) or its famous Carnival being featured on Saturday afternoon telly, sandwiched between the regular diet of all-in wrestling, show jumping and boat racing.

On the basis that any old excuse would do (from a bank holiday to a coronation), the TV companies would rush instantly, van loads of cameras and miles of cable to any likely festive vantage point, but not *too* far from London. Nationwide television was still a few years away and in the mid-1950s, ITV was several Companies short of a network.

The actual subject seemed not to matter. Everything was new and it was all grist to the TV mill. Indeed, for years, a South-

end seafront gypsy fortune-teller had a sign displayed which read proudly: 'As featured on BBC Television'. Doubtless the seekers of fortune were suitably impressed.

Southend 1956, Carnival Camera

But it was Southend Carnival that provided the ultimate black and white TV attraction. In 1956, the commercial company ATV transmitted the festivities, setting up their cameras and control vans beside the old swimming pool at nearby Westcliff. Included in the day's programme was a beauty contest (typical ITV) from the pool. Later in the afternoon, a proportion of the carnival procession was televised. For this, two cameras were used, one mounted on a dolly beside the road and the other, high on a gantry using a new-fangled zoom lens. What all these Southend programmes ac-

tually looked like, I now have only fragmentary recollections. Old TV-Timers will tell you that these O.B.s were fraught with technical and artistic problems. Cameras would focus on the wrong item or break down at critical moments. Commentators would lose their sound-leads or drop their microphones. Interviewees would freeze-up in panic and forget their own names. Strange and inexplicable pauses proliferated. Everything over-ran. And it always seemed to be raining.

Television outside broadcasting was not new. It began as far back as the early 1930s. On May 8th 1931, Scottish innovator, John Logie Baird loaded a mechanical 30-line picture scanner into a wood holiday caravan, trundled this into the street outside his London Long Acre workshop and relayed (if only across a few yards) an image from 'outside'. Later, that same year on June 3rd, Baird took his TV caravan down to Epsom and broadcast live scenes from the Derby (the first sports O.B.) via the BBC medium wave transmitter at Brookman's Park. A bold technological feat considering the totally uncharted TV territory and the haphazard nature of the telephone lines that linked the system. The pictures of the Derby (actually just the winning post area) were barely recognisable (viewers thought the horses looked like blurred camels). The poor image quality was due to electrical interference and the low bandwidth used. But a precedent had been established. O.B.s worked! Although Baird's creaky TV system was abandoned ultimately as impractical, the publicity value of such demonstrations spurred further developments, especially in all-electronic television.

Elsewhere in Europe, at the 1936 Berlin Olympic Games, the German experimental TV service used two O.B. vans feeding a mixture of 180-line electronic and semi-live intermediate-film pictures (film shot first then quickly developed – very quickly, about 45 seconds – and then passed through a scanner beam). But the first *all-electronic* high definition 405-line outside broadcast unit was built in 1937 for BBC Television. The unit comprised two Regal vans built by AEC of Southall and equipped by the Marconi-EMI company. A third vehicle carried the 1kw VHF link transmitter. The unit supplied all the necessary control apparatus. This included two vision monitors and four microphone inputs. Three

Dicky with Fred Quilly and Mum at Clacton, 1956

'Emitron' cameras supplied the pictures and on May 12th 1937 the unit televised live the coronation procession of King George VI. With outside broadcasts such as described, early television established an audience, and importantly, sold sets.

Unfortunately, no official recordings exist of any of those pre-war transmissions (there does reside somewhere in the BBC archives a brief snatch of blurry amateur footage showing the 1937 coronation broadcast filmed off the screen. This was taken by a Marconi employee using his own 16mm camera) and likewise none of the 1950s Southend Carnival outside broadcasts. They were not exactly historic, nor considered at the time worthy of any sort of archive preservation. My memories of that 1956 Southend Carnival are reinforced by the photographs my father and I took of the television technical gear. But I shall always recall, fondly, the remark made to me by an ATV cameraman who was filming the carnival. As a TV camera-mad twelve year old, I confessed to him that I wanted to be a TV cameraman when I grew up. 'Bugger off, can't you see I'm working?' he muttered helpfully. But I wasn't abashed by these pearls of advice. It was but a mere forty years later that I actually achieved my ambition.

And so it transpired that during the entire 1950s, a spotty telly-potty kid was I, inflicted with a strange yearn for a taste of TV technology: the camera, the lights, the studio, the lot. I applied regularly for free audience tickets to BBC television variety productions (ITV studios had a higher audience age limit of sixteen years, thus I was then too young to enter, so BBC shows it had to be). They included *The Ted Ray Show* and *The Billy Cotton Band Show*. These, not particularly popular concoctions, were produced live and dripping from an old converted West London theatre, the Shepherd's Bush Empire, on Shepherd's Bush Green.

A visit to the Empire (renamed in 1953, the BBC Television Theatre) was always an adventure, a trip to the Big Bad City and a chance to see real TV cameras in action! For an impressionable nipper, it was an exciting time, full of mystery and wonder. On arrival at the Television Theatre I would join the queue, clutching my dedicated BBC ticket. I always liked to arrive early, because it was first come, first served in the allocation of seats. I hoped for a front

row pew from whence I could ogle all the technical telly action. As I nursed youthful dreams of becoming a TV cameraman, I considered these studio trips an educational outing; a learning curve.

Outside the Television Theatre, during the forty minutes-or-so queuing time, the programme's 'stars' would sometimes wander out for a breather, or perhaps to size up the audience? (More probably they were hoping to elicit admiring stares). Ever on the lookout for excitement, I once took my Box Brownie and photographed comedian Terry Scott and singer Alan Breeze (of the *Billy Cotton Band Show*). Also, I snapped a surprised BBC technician who got his picture taken just because he *looked* famous.

Terry Scott outside the Television Theatre, 1958.

Another feature of the Television Theatre queue was the professional beggars. In those days there were two them. The-Busker-with-the-Trumpet and The-Blind-Man-with-the-Matches. The-Blind-Man-with-the-Matches did absolutely nothing, instead he shuffled along the queue (with the help of his wife) muttering 'blind, blind', and offering matches from his tray in exchange for

donations. Not very entertaining. Next came The-Busker-with-the-Trumpet. He would suddenly blast out, more-or-less in key, several excruciating and totally unrecognisable tunes. When he'd finished his act, he also proceeded along the queue in search of funds. The routine was always the same. Blind first, then the Totally Tone Deaf. It was a relief to get inside the theatre. And the television cameras were a revelation.

The Television Theatre was equipped with four Marconi-made cameras. These large TV cameras produced dynamic 405-line monochrome pictures with comparatively little light. I had anticipated vast searchlights dazzling everything in the studio. In fact the illumination was quite restrained and logically directed using banks of quite small spot lights and various circular flood lamps named, quaintly, Scoops.

Those early TV shows, however, appeared far better in the flesh than they appeared on the screen at home. At the time, BBC light entertainment (as opposed presumably, to BBC *heavy* entertainment) ran a very poor second – with less than 30% of the audience – to the glamorous and flashy ITV. However, the most noticeable and startling to anyone new to the sight of a television studio was the sheer *colour* of it all. Also the clear, vibrant quality of the live audio.

In fact, strange to relate, those old-time TV stars were not instantly recognisable in the flesh, so used as we were to viewing them in 'glorious' black and white. My mum (who accompanied me to several shows) was utterly convinced that a handsome BBC stagehand was pianist Russ Conway. Whereas all the while, the *real* Russ Conway, known for his twinkling smile and full front set, was sitting dumpy, hunched and unglamorous at the side of the stage awaiting his cue. When Russ come on to play a tune, my Mum actually thought *he* was an impostor, because he didn't 'look' anything like his appearance on the home screen!

Such was the power of television in those days, performers were regarded reverentially, as some sort of super-beings from outer space, and not like real people at all. Things haven't changed much.

CHAPTER 2

Some Finished Artwork

Time to leave school, and so with absolutely no academic qualifications whatsoever, what to do? In 1959, and this is true, there were jobs aplenty. Oh yes. A friend at the time changed jobs every week! Here was me with nothing to offer but a clutch of artless *Superman* cartoons, but I was very keen to learn. And so, with very little effort, I gained employment in London at £4 a week as an office boy in a small advertising art studio called Pentagon Design Services. This outfit had premises in Rupert Street, Soho, W1.

Pentagon Design Services consisted of three febrile and cramped floors of closet pederasts, neo-Nazis and dipsy Scotsmen. Naturally, I was oblivious to the implications of all this. I was, after all, only fifteen years old and had never before met a real Scotsman. Rupert Street was on the edge of London's Theatre-Land and the place abounded with 'colourful' characters, including a coffee bar pædophile who used to regularly try and tempt me (unsuccessfully) by producing something out of his trouser pocket, but it was only a chunk of amber with a fly trapped in it.

Some mornings, when I arrived for work, the street would be littered with drunks and sad to say, our little design studio regularly had its early morning doorstep milk delivery nicked by op-

Early cartoon of Pentagon Design Services Staff, 1960.

Pentagon Studio.

Sorting negs, 1959.

Soho scene, 1961.

portunistic and thirsty derelicts. Further into the working day and groups of strolling tinker street musicians would wander down Rupert Street. These melodious minstrels received our undivided attention. A favourite trick was to hurl pennies down to their outstretched hands ('tank you soor...') but first we fully-heated the coins to cherry red over our kettle gas ring. Another juvenile jape was to squirt lighter fluid under the lavatory door (when occupied by colleagues) then light and retire. At other idle moments we played darts. Our skills were variable, culminating once in a well-placed missile imbedding itself, double top, into somebody's thigh.

My daily working routine consisted of ferrying around London, artwork produced by the studio (nothing very elaborate, just small illustrations for patent pharmaceuticals or kitchen cutlery) to various clients. Occasionally, l took artwork to the commercial television companies. All this was very exciting. At the time, they had premises in Hanover Square (ABC TV), Golden Square (Granada TV) and Great Cumberland Place (ATV) Sometimes l delivered material to an imposing ITV building in Kingsway (once called Adastral House, formally home to the Air Ministry) and now aptly rechristened Television House. This was the home of Associated-Rediffusion Ltd (it also contained the studios of ITN plus an office for Scottish Television). Very glam – lots of potted plants, sleek decor and even sleeker lady receptionists! Heaven.

The advertising artwork that l diligently transported consisted of short messages, (perhaps illustrated), constructed as 10x12 inch captions used in 'spot' commercials. It was simple, direct stuff. No fancy video shoots or clever angles. Just a bit of cardboard, but cardboard or not, it certainly made money for everyone, especially the television companies. For example, back in 1961 one could purchase from ATV (in the Midlands) a five second slide, with announcer's voice-over, on the afternoon show *Lunch Box* for fifteen quid. At peak times the cost of an ATV five second slot rocketed to a staggering £70! By way of financial contrast, the *all-day* five second price on Ulster Television was a mere £8. ABC TV by comparison would charge for five seconds a weekend top rate (Sunday evenings) of £576. But that was the cheaper end of the television advertising market. The expensive stuff (at 1961 prices in

the London or Midlands area) ran at an average £1,000 for an ordinary 30 second peak-time airing of a professionally filmed commercial which had probably cost at least £5,000 to make.

Quite soon, I was promoted, from office boy to negative-sorter. The top floor of Pentagon Design Services had a small photographic department run by a rabid anti-Semite (he claimed – amongst other racist things – that Jewish tailors were no big deal and so he set about, and indeed succeeded, in making his own bespoke sports coat). Eric, for that was his name, also had a phobia about being photographed. Ironic for a photographer, one would have thought? But Eric died soon after of lung cancer (not as a direct result of his bigotry I hasten to add) and so I moved up a notch. I was again promoted, this time to the running of the D&P (Develop and Print) section. I got so proficient I could actually develop and print without the need of timers or measures. It became almost second nature (A skill curiously now no longer required since the advent of digital photography).

Lunch hours (plus sandwiches) were spent in various West End News Theatres, a now long-abandoned form of cinema that showed the 'latest' newsreels from Pathe, Gaumont British, or Movietone News. Padding the 'News' programme was a string of elderly comedy 'shorts' from beyond the Hollywood grave. *The Three Stooges* or *Laurel and Hardy*, plus cartoons from Disney. Also MGM's *Tom and Jerry* or Warner's, *Tweety Pie and Sylvester* (the best). I sat through my very favourite, a Chuck Jones classic called *One Froggy Evening* about twenty times, soggy sandwiches forgotten.

Thus cartoons were never far away. I was still scribbling in my spare time and I must confess that to this day, I'm not certain who suggested I try and actually *sell* my cartoons. Newspapers in our house were the *Daily Mirror*, and the *Daily Sketch* with the weekly *TV Times*, all of which had glorious cartoon pages displaying the works of cartoonists with curious signatures like 'Clew', 'Chic', 'Waller', 'Whimsy' or 'Styx'. So I gave it a try and submitted a few 'single' cartoons. My cartoon jokes were pretty standard for the time, mothers-in-law, wives, policemen, stupid kids, that sort of thing and my cartoon style of drawing was very awkward and undistinguished. Nothing sold for a few months, and then, Bang!

19

A sale! My very first and it was to the *TV Times*. My cartoon was printed in their 'Natural Break' cartoon page. I was paid the fabulous sum of three guineas. It was 1962 and I was well and truly on my way.

TV Times *Natural Break*.

However, as a photographer, I was still learning my trade. I would often take my lovely Yashica Mat twin lens reflex camera (poor man's Rollieflex) out and about, loaded with a roll of Ilford HP3 120 film. I still have, filed away, some nice shots in and around Liverpool Street Station, Piccadilly Circus and the River Thames at night, all historic views now. I also took several Soho scenes featuring the occasional celebrity wandering the streets. David Frost was one such, plus a hasty snap of a curious looking exhibitionist being hauled along in a cart. The exhibitionist I later identified as a (then) nonentity called Jimmy Savile. He was being trundled around London for a St Albans Student Rag Week. Little did we know... but at the time I was just snapping away with no thought of future times and events. I printed all my own work

and the processing was free. However, the job at Pentagon was beginning to pawl. I was reaching that stage when something new seemed to beckon, and that something new was BBC2.

David Frost in Soho, 1963.

Savile, 1962.

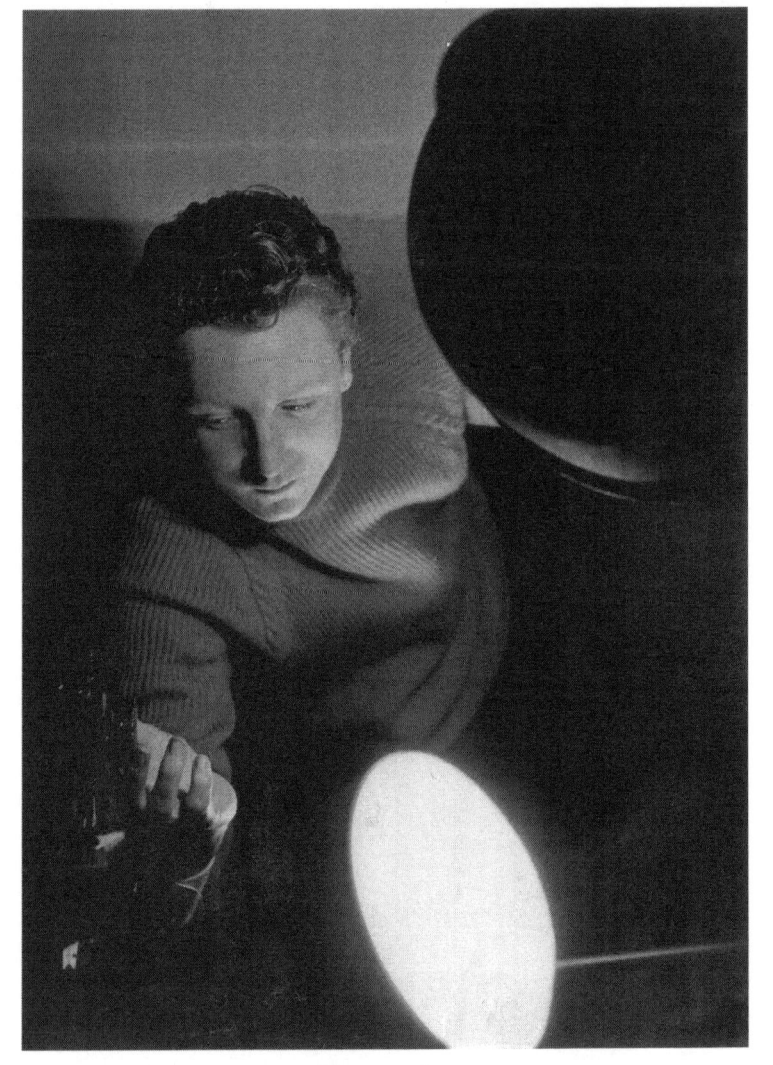

Photographer.

Life drawing, 1962.

23

CHAPTER 3

Screen Test

The BBC had been granted a second television channel which opened on April 20th 1964, so popular on the night it blew all the lights in West London. They were fast recruiting staff and I answered an advertisement in a trade journal seeking anyone interested. I do mean *anyone*. In past times, the old civil service-style BBC had insisted on a few qualifications, basic school certificates etc. I had none. However, never tardy about hiding my bushel under a light, I applied for a post as a 'film assistant', citing my previous professional photographic work and also my precocious ventures into amateur 16mm filming. I explained that I had shot a few scenes at the 1961 Radio Show at Earls Court when the BBC had first shown colour TV to the public at large (this footage can now be seen in its entirety somewhere on YouTube). I neglected to mention in my application that I would have gaily sawn off my right leg to become a BBC Television employee!

So it came to pass that I started my first BBC job (with all limbs intact) on March 16th 1964 for the grand yearly sum of £690. I had to get a bank account and even wear a tie. I was employed as a 'Trainee Film Assistant' and I travelled each day from Harold Wood in Essex to Ealing Film Studios, a daily round trip door-to-

door of approximately four hours. But did I care? Hey, I was working at the BBC! Not exactly BBC *Television*, indeed I never, during my brief BBC career, worked at Lime Grove, Riverside or Television Centre. I was based at Ealing, or as the BBC entitled it 'TFS' (Television Film Studios). But at least it had the word *Television* in the title and I did get to meet a Dalek.

CHAPTER 4

On Ealing Green

In 1955, the BBC bought the famous Ealing Film Studios and in 1956 transferred all their film 'effort' as they liked to term it. At the time, BBC Television used a vast quantity of film which included film inserts to live programming like *Z Cars* or *Tonight*. Also nature footage for wildlife productions with David Attenborough or special documentaries (Elgar, Debussy) for *Monitor*, directed by luminaries such as Ken Russell. During my time at Ealing the biggest production progressing was a vast landmark 26-episode BBC2 series called *The Great War*. Sardonic comments by staff indicated that this production was taking more resources to produce and finish than the Great War itself.

Ealing boasted three large production studios, thirty two cutting rooms, lighting and camera departments, a film vault, a dubbing theatre and a film review suite, which is where I worked. Me and my colleagues ran projectors and sound reproducers, showing various bits of film footage including rushes, complete programmes or library appraisals. BBC film cameraman Nat Crosby reckoned we were all 'young enthusiasts' waiting for an opportunity to graduate to the camera department. Maybe that was the case, but for the time being it was nice just standing around being

paid to watch movies all day long. Initially our Bell & Howell 609 projectors used carbon arc lamps, (which needed trimming and watching to make certain the 'arc' gap didn't get too wide) but soon changed to Xenon lamps for an easier working life. Also by the mid-1960s, 16mm film was supplanting the use of 35mm in television production and so gradually, all our 35mm projectors (bar two) were replaced.

The 'Dalek' episode was somewhat unremarkable, inasmuch as an inert wood and tin TV prop frightens absolutely nobody, with the exception of a small child (on a staff family visit) who steadfastly refused to venture any further past the props shed where the aforementioned Skaroan was temporarily and visibly housed. It transpired that the Dalek was on day-release from Television Centre. It was going to be filmed for an insert into a BBC2 *Out of the Unknown* drama entitled *Get Off Of My Cloud*, an episode now sadly missing from the BBC archives.

CHAPTER 5

Hits and Misses

The 'BBC Club' was a great BBC institution, a watering hole for the Corporation-stressed and their guests. To be sure, very little *water* was necessarily consumed, but a visit to 'the Club', (apart from attempting to impress young ladies), was an opportunity to visit BBC television studios and in particular the fabulous Television Centre at White City.

The late-lamented Centre (foolishly sold in 2013 for a mere pittance by the BBC's Head of Bad Moves & National Disgraces) was designed by a true genius architect (Graham Dawbarn) who thoughtfully included in the ring doughnut-shaped building, studio viewing galleries to all the main production areas. Thus, on my various TVC trips I would nonchalantly wander around, peer down and observe rehearsals and recordings.

Doctor Who and the Sensorites was one such. This was being recorded in Studio 3 with William Hartnell and Carole Ann Ford, whom I distinctly recall 'dancing' about as the end music played and the captions rolled. I apprised Carole of this memory when I met her in 2013 during my filming on the set of the BBC commemorative *Doctor Who* drama, *An Adventure in Space and Time*. Naturally, Carole had no recollection of her impromptu jig,

but was thrilled that I had remembered something so trivial.

One of the perks of BBC employment was priority access to tickets for light entertainment or other programmes requiring an audience. Applications for popular shows were usually oversubscribed, but BBC staff got advance warning of what was coming and so we could all jump the 'queue'. As a result of gaining one of these tickets, I actually appeared for the very first time on television. The programme was a cheap and cheerful production called *Juke Box Jury*.

Juke Box Jury.

Juke Box Jury wasn't the most original BBC television programme of the 1960s, but it was certainly one of the most popular and it had a secret ingredient in the shape of, The General Public. *Juke Box Jury*, chaired by genial David Jacobs, first aired in 1959. Initially, it occupied an early evening weekday slot but later, the show was shifted to Saturday peak time in order to compete with ITV's frantic (and innovative) pop show *Boy Meets Girl*. Like most British popular TV programmes of the time, *Juke Box Jury* was adapted from an American original format.

During 1953 in Hollywood, station KNXT (a CBS affiliate) first transmitted the programme, devised and hosted by an engaging character called Peter Potter. The KNXT show, sponsored each week by a variety of products, concentrated on the (usually six) star guests and even had a live music spot. The *raison d'être* of the show was that the celebrity panel displayed their ignorance, wit or judgement about various newly-released popular recorded ditties. Also, the US version had a glamorous 'hostess', who during the playing of the discs, wandered amongst the jurists dispensing 'refreshments'.

The BBC's version of *Juke Box Jury* had fewer jurists (four), and no glamour girl dishing out BBC plonk. The main departure from the US format was that during the disc play, the cameras concentrated on the studio audience, therein laid the success and popular appeal of the programme. People clamoured for tickets just for a chance to be 'on the telly', albeit only for five seconds a shot.

Juke Box Jury was staged at several of the BBC's studio sites, including the Television Theatre at Shepherd's Bush, Lime Grove Studio G and Television Centre Studio 2. It is true that elderly BBC studio commissionaires always had to stand well clear when the audience was admitted because usually there was an almighty stampede for the front row. This was somewhat pointless as the cameras always found faces to shoot wherever they were seated. No amount of admonishing, 'Don't rush, don't rush!' made the slightest difference.

Juke Box Jury was broadcast ostensibly 'live' each Saturday, but what actually occurred was that after the live show was aired, another was recorded. To facilitate this, the audience was judiciously shuffled, the panel changed, the Juke Box re-stuffed and off we went again. This meant of course, that when a lucky member of the audience got 'caught' on camera during the *recorded* show they could catch up with their star performance the following week. This is exactly what happened to me. The following week I had my camera trained on the TV screen and managed to capture a frame of my less than riveting performance as 'a member of the audience'.

On one occasion at the Television Theatre, (I was in the studio again) at the end of the live broadcast, the cameras were kept

trained on the audience. As the cameras panned about focussing on individuals, this caused a *frisson* around the theatre. It transpired subsequently that a policeman had seen the live broadcast and thought he had spotted a 'wanted' face amongst the audience, though this later turned out not to be the case. Thus was the power of live television. This was the days of only three channels, black and white images, and of course no home video tape recorders. Indeed it now appears that the police missed a trick searching for potential criminals because one of the 'Jurors' that day was the 'nonentity' Jimmy Savile.

Juke Box Jury (even the signature tune was a hit) ended its original BBC run in 1967. The programme resurfaced in 1979 with Noel Edmonds and again in 1989 with Jools Holland honking the hooter, but the original excitement had vanished. It was impossible to recapture those special magic TV moments such as when all four Beatles and later the Rolling Stones were 'jurists'. (all recordings, of course, usefully missing from the BBC archives). And then there was the time when singer Johnny Mathis stuck a clothes peg on his nose in a witty attempt to characterise the 'quality' of a Cliff Richard song. Soon after, Mathis' career in this country went into a bit of a decline.

CHAPTER 6

Time at the Palace

Journeying westwards to Ealing every week was beginning to irk. Also, I was at an age when I decided it might be quite nice to live away from home. My current weekly wage was around £15 per week so I could easily afford a bedsit room somewhere nearby. Indeed, what actually happened was that I shifted BBC locations entirely and re-established myself in North London, high atop a hill near Alexandra Palace.

Alexandra Palace (or 'AP' in BBC parlance) was currently the home of Television News. The two original pre-war BBC production studios had closed in 1954, only to be re-inhabited by the fledgling BBC television news organisation. Initially, BBC TV News had run a very poor second to the dynamic ITN, but by the mid-1960s (when I turned up) things had improved. Richard Baker, Robert Dougall, Michael Aspel and Peter Woods were the 'newsreaders' and very much the stars of the show. I on the other hand was still running projectors, stuck, single-handed in shanty booths, spooling 16mm news footage in very short chunks for the assembled film editors to assess. I can't say that this was the most interesting aspect of my BBC career. Fortunately, several other BBC employees were members of the Finchley Amateur Cine Society, and as I now

owned a superior Bolex H16 16mm cine camera I became involved in shooting some of the Society's homemade movie projects.

One dramatic presentation was called *Ivorypaws* and for this epic I shot some footage flying in a light aircraft (looking down on the 'baddies' running around in a field). I also drew and filmed, frame-by-frame, an animated title sequence which was my first and last venture into *Looney Tunes* territory. Not content with a backstage role, I also 'acted' in another amateur offering (*Ratman and Bobbin* – guess what *that* was all about). For this I had to pretend to be a pop singer miming away on a stage with my 'group' behind me. I roped in a friend, Christopher Priest to appear in the 'band'. Christopher Priest is now an award-winning and highly respected author of science fiction, so it didn't do him any harm. All this merry 16mm filming didn't come cheap. Fortunately, BBC TV News had its own on-site film developing and processing plant, and so naturally, us Finchley Filmsters took advantage of this facility, quite a few times if I recall.

But I was still submitting cartoons to all and sundry, and doing quite well too getting into *The Sun*, *The Daily Sketch*, *Titbits*, *Reveille*, *News of the World*. My BBC bosses weren't too pleased with me because 'established' BBC staffers were not supposed to have 'second jobs' (but I knew for a fact that at least one film editor owned a travel agency and another made quite rude films). Eventually, I tried to perk up my working life by changing BBC jobs. I applied for a post as a trainee news film editor, which I attained, but soon lost interest in the truly tedious process of cutting bits of film to a length 15 seconds (or less) and so with some regret, in November 1968 I resigned from the BBC. I cashed in my entire BBC pension contributions (£234.18.11d) and left the Corporation for good.

Oh, did I mention a few lines back, 'rude films'. It goes without saying, (and perhaps it should), that it was not unknown for my steamy projection booth to whirr away occasionally to an engrossed audience, the flickering screen displaying some positively untransmittable images. Next up: nothing much. Just getting married and continuing the path towards my 'Destiny' as a freelance cartoonist. So what could *possibly* go wrong?

Movie director.

With Bolex H16.

Dicky as pop singer.

CHAPTER 7

Spots and Strips

It was 1969 and I was full of optimism. I had married lovely Margaret, whose parents were Buckinghamshire middle class tax collector Tories. And me, a council house boy from Ravensbourne Crescent (sometimes called Rogues Crescent) so they weren't best-pleased to have in the family an out-of-work, sarcastic, artistic scruff. However, blithely ignoring all that, we set up home in a first floor rented flat at 19a Birdhurst Road, South Croydon. Handy for the railway station too, which was nearby with London only twenty minutes door to door.

I was on my way (or so I thought). First call, *The Daily Mirror*. I had been selling single cartoons to the paper for a few years. Not bad money but not regular. What I needed was a coveted daily contract (or even weekly) to produce a strip cartoon. I roughed out some thoughts and developed an idea (not very original, as it turned out) which, I reasoned, was right up their Fleet Street. *Space Flot* was the title, a 'funny' science research lab with a mad professor, a dippy scientist, an odd-job man and a lab dog who uttered nothing but 'Yip'.

'Nope' was the *Mirror*'s reaction. I tried again with other ideas, even one about a talking blob of shaving cream called, with

faultless logic, 'Blob'. But the main nationals (even tried to interest *The Times*) were having none of it, or me. To have landed a daily cartoon strip would have earned me quite a bit of kudos and cash. To put that into context, pre-eminent cartoonist Bill Tidy began in 1971 a *Daily Mirror* strip entitled *The Fosdyke Saga*. Bill was interviewed on the BBC's *World At One* by William Hardcastle, who intimated that Bill could now afford to own an Aston Martin DB4! Such dreams.

I continued to sell 'singles', or what was termed 'spot' cartoons. Some publications paid nine guineas, some two quid. But the market then was quite large so there were ample opportunities to make sales. For example, the national red tops had a daily cartoon page, with the *Daily Sketch* having the best. Weekly magazines had them too including *Titbits*, *Reveille*, *Weekend*, *TV Times*, and D.C. Thomson's *Weekly News* (one of the worst pay rates by the way). My total earnings for 1969 were £807 or about fifteen quid a week. But let us leave the heady world of cartoons for a moment and zoom off into Outer Space.

First car with Margaret, first and last wife.

Birdhurst Road, 1969.

CHAPTER 8

Science Fiction & Sky Watching

During the 1960s I discovered the delights of science fiction (or SF as correctly termed, *never* the pejorative 'Sci-Fi'). There existed at the time (and still does) an organisation called The British Science Fiction Association. This Association was fan-based, but with a notable coterie of professional writers. SF fans would socialise at regular intervals and, once a year, would attend (usually at Easter) Conventions dotted around the UK. It was a fun time of lectures by authors, book sales, art shows, fancy dress and booze. Mainly booze. Several BSFA members produced amateur magazines called fanzines, (a creative way of communicating before the era of blogs, Facebook and other internet blessings). Most of these fanzine publications (produced using wax stencils and churned out on Gestetner rotary printers), were execrable, but a few had genuine merit, indeed, several future SF authors contributed as young fans, learning their craft. I had a go too, drawing cartoons and illustrations directly onto these wax stencils, which required a good degree of pre-planning and a steady hand. The results were quite satisfying.

I produced my first science fiction 'fanzine' in 1964, and contributed most of the written and drawn contents. One feature was a short and simple-minded critique of the relatively new television

SF programme *Doctor Who*. The article was entitled, somewhat misleadingly, 'A Rocket For *Doctor Who*'. For your delectation, this is the full text:

> '*Compulsive nonsense*' *is what a university lecturer called the* Doctor Who *series in the press the other day. To quote, 'the weird adventures in time and space of the BBC1 children's series* Doctor Who *left Edward Blishen of York University cold'.*
>
> *The fact that the said lecturer watched the programme proves something, but is, in fact* Doctor Who *such nonsense as he claims it to be? For the child audience, this programme is one of the better in the way of small-budget productions. Its popularity shows this to be the case, and all in all,* Doctor Who *is good, clean fun, if a little simple in outlook. The overall dialogue could be improved as could the flimsy story lines, but taking all into account, this programme is unpretentious. Some claim that it is also educational and this is true to an extent, although much of this education is in itself confused. The back-drops of the production may range from Marco Polo to the Aztecs and there may be occasional date-dropping to set the scene, but these are all asides. We just have a lashing of pseudo-science to help the action along and if a Dalek gets in the way, we just invent a ray gun to deal with it. Some adult SF is in this mould. Never-the-less for children, and a great many adults, myself included,* Doctor Who *is entertaining and any demerits it may have are lost in the overall production. To call* Doctor Who *compulsive nonsense is, I feel non-productive. Mr Blishen might as well write off the whole of TV in its present form as to damn one small children's programme. As for leaving the said gentlemen 'cold' well after all sir, the programme wasn't designed for your age group.*

Not one of my more erudite articles perhaps, but it was a start. I had also vague dreams of becoming a science fiction writer myself. I went as far as taking a postal writing course which actually

pooh-poohed science fiction as a genre. The instructors were adamant that I should first become proficient at 'proper' writing before attempting anything stupid. I buckled down and actually learnt a few things, such as getting a 'hook' in early to interest the reader. My main difficulty was that I couldn't think of any interesting stories to tell or work out a proper plot. I did actually manage to sell one short story entitled *The Haul*, to *Titbits* magazine. It was co-written with chum Chris Priest (a proper writer). The story was a slice of whimsy concerning an unlucky burglar called Gerry who was foiled stealing a thousand quid life savings from under a bed because it was all in threepenny pieces!

At the time, my favourite SF authors were Bob Shaw, Robert Heinlein, Arthur C. Clarke, Brian Aldiss, Harry Harrison. Phillip K. Dick and Robert Sheckley (and fifty years later they are still). For a relative youngster, science fiction clubdom was good fun and, as intimated, several SF fans went on to greater things; Terry Pratchett, Christopher Priest, Mike Ashley, Malcolm Edwards *et al* achieved deserved success as writers, editors or journalists within the genre.

During the mid-1960s there was a flurry of British flying saucer reports. Newspapers published accounts of weird bangs and other loud noises with sightings of strange nocturnal lights in the sky. Photos soon appeared, one depicted an object looking like a flying eye and another of a large alien dish-shaped object resting in a field with a policeman looking at it. As an avid reader of science fiction, this spiked my interest and I began to delve into the subject. A group of local flying saucer enthusiasts had their base in Wood Green near to Muswell Hill where I had my bedsit. I was invited to attend what they termed a 'Sky Watch'. A nearby open space called Crews Hill was chosen to be thus watched from, and so we all trouped up one dark evening to watch the sky. Negative results, apart from a bit of rain. But my enthusiasm for the subject was never knowingly dampened and this inevitably lead me to the delightful Wiltshire town of Warminster. Now Warminster, during the 1960s, had apparently, a non-stop parade of strange aerial objects flitting about with seemingly gay abandon. I delved further.

High in the Warminster UFO firmament was a local West

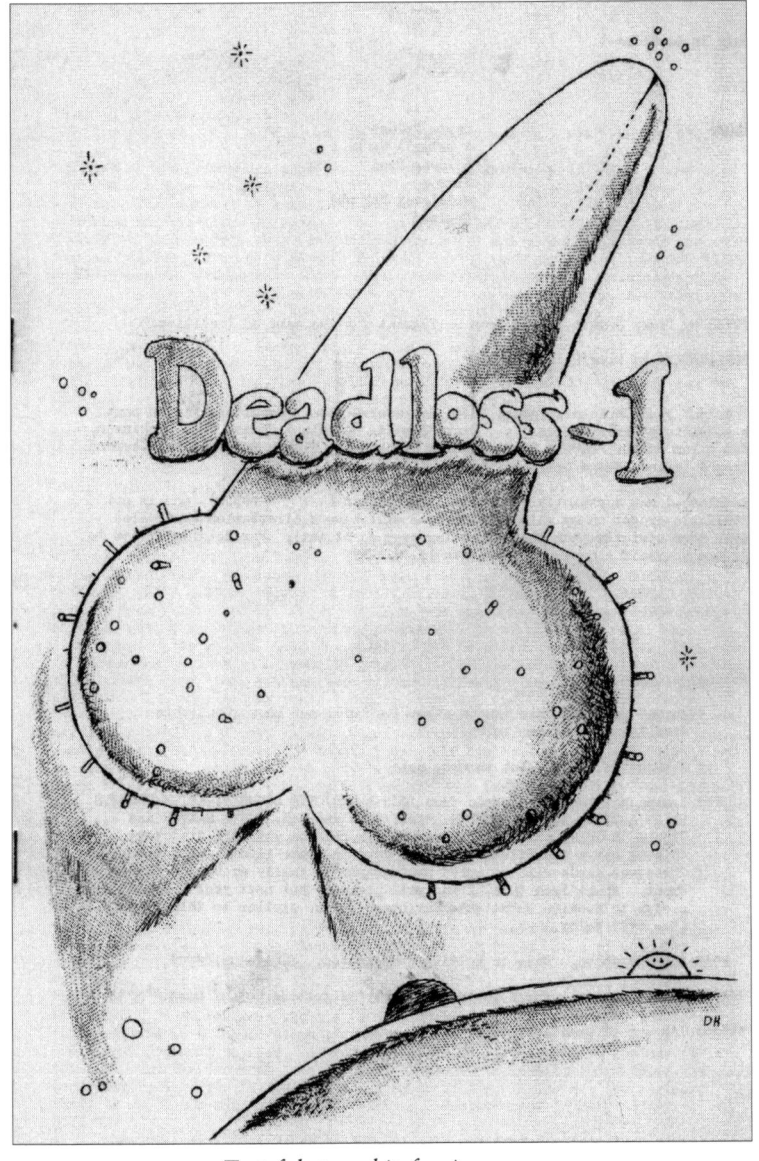

Tasteful spaceship fanzine cover.

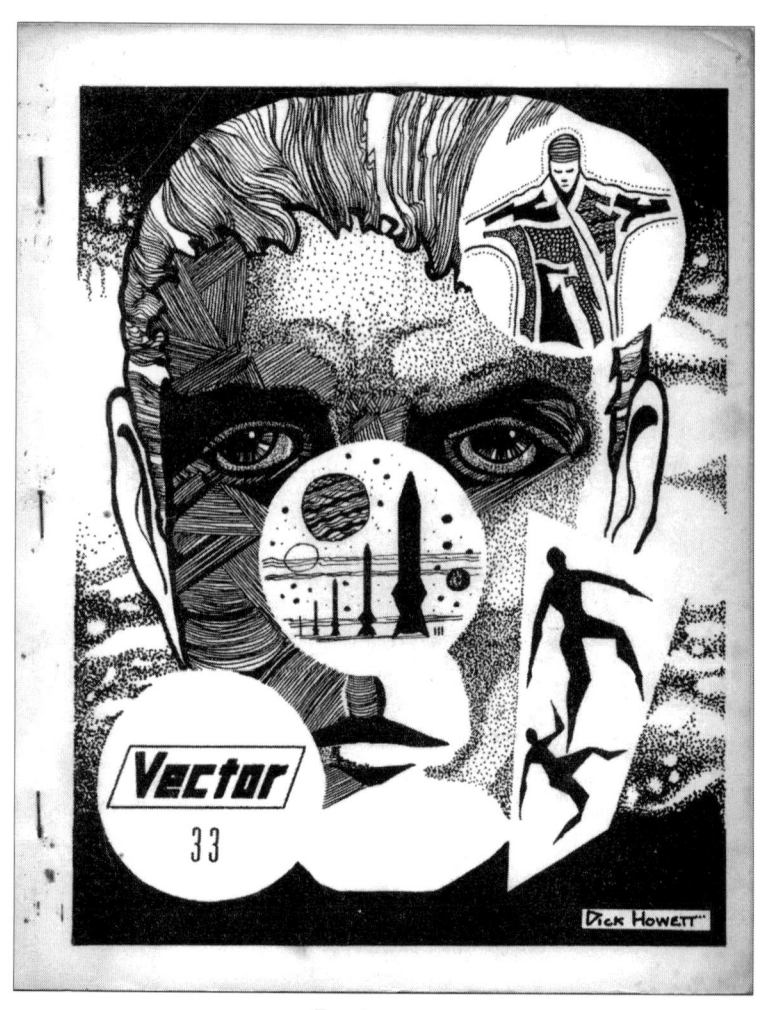

Fanzine cover.

Country journalist named Arthur Shuttlewood. After an alleged bout of scepticism, Arthur nailed firmly his reporting skills to the worldwide interest in the Warminster Flying Saucer or 'Thing' as it was dubbed. Arthur became a convert to the cause. He was an engaging and garrulous individual and he expounded, to anyone who would listen, an entirely plausible case for the entire Flying Saucer phenomenon. He did this at regular intervals, usually to a small but rapt audience, all waiting to get a word in edgeways. His entertaining book, *The Warminster Mystery* became an immediate bestseller.

I had never seen a UFO and so in 1967 I travelled to Warminster in the hope of revelations. I took along my 16mm Bolex movie camera to make a 'sky watch' film about, (as it transpired), a group of people wandering around on a hill, not seeing a UFO. My film was called *The Warminster Watch*. It was shown later to a packed audience at the Caxton Hall in London (a rather scratched copy can now be viewed on YouTube) and it featured Arthur and chums waving telescopes and 'UFO detectors' across the Wiltshire skyline in the hope of seeing the elusive 'Thing'. Local landmark Cradle Hill was the sky watching hot spot, but no spots, hot or otherwise, were seen. Later, local BBC Television arrived to cover the event, and later I distinctly heard the cameraman mutter to his producer that we were all 'a bunch of bloody loonies'.

With that endorsement ringing in my ears, my next close encounter with UFOs was on a fan discussion panel at a science fiction convention. I was inveigled to sit on this panel and found myself next to author Michael Moorcock, an imposing, opinionated and popular writer of science fiction. Sitting alongside a few others (offering no support I might add) there was lonely old me up there to argue the case of 'Why Flying Saucers?' This was the panel title, listed in the programme of Convention Events.

I came armed with notes, evidence and other bits and bobs to convince the sceptic. At the last moment I couldn't find them, which didn't help the nervous twitch I had developed during the course of the morning. Mike Moorcock spread his colours early, adopting his characteristic reasoned approach. 'Mass hysteria,' he opined, 'War psychosis,' he added, a phrase he had pinched from

the Russians. 'People don't *really* see flying saucers, they're worried about the Vietnam war.' The rest of the panel mumbled in agreement. I was outnumbered. I looked again for my notes. 'It's a chain reaction you see,' Mike continued. 'People read about UFOs in the paper and then go out and *imagine* they see them.'

I was asked for my opinion. 'I believe in the existence of space machines from other worlds,' I cried, 'Why not? What is wrong with that admission?'

Well *everything*, according to Mike. 'War psychosis,' he reiterated. 'The biggest amounts of sightings occur when the population is concerned about its personal safety. People are worried about the Bomb too.'

At that point I lapsed into a resigned silence. Understandable, when the rest of the panel, plus the formidable Mike Moorcock, had such cut and dried explanations to parry with. Besides I needed time to reflect upon my newly acquired war psychosis.

Dicky and Mike Moorcock on the UFO panel.

47

CHAPTER 9

Cartoons Again and
Radical Thoughts

It was now 1971 and I was drifting along with quite a few published cartoons and also a few strips. Yes, I had made the small time at last! Several weekly and monthly efforts including, *Hi Fi Hector* in a Hi Fi magazine *Video Vic* in a video magazine and *Movie Millie – Queen of the Hard "Cors"* in a very rude magazine (but more of that later). Another strip, *Office Hours* ran for a few years in an industry trade magazine (for the computer fraternity) called *Datalink*. I've added this to the list because my wife Margaret supplied me with ideas for this strip. Indeed she *appears* in it! The 'office' in question was the IT department of a lightly disguised City stockbroker firm called Phillips & Drew where Margaret was employed as a computer programmer. Nobody twigged (or cared) but the strip ran for quite a few years and it was good money too.

During 1971, we bid farewell to South Croydon. Margaret and myself scraped together a deposit, enough towards an £8,000 mortgage (oh, the good old days) and bought an end of terrace three-bedroomed town house in Chelmsford, Essex. Why Chelmsford? Draw a circle on a map and work outwards taking note of property prices. Bit cheaper the further the circle spread. Which brings me to CRAB.

Office Hours *in* Datalink, *1978.*

CRAB *magazine.*

CRAB *magazine.*

Now, CRAB was the Chelmsford Radical Bulletin (whose acronym should have actually been CRB). Anyway, my involvement began when I visited the opticians for an eye check and new specs. I was obliged to give my occupation, 'Ah, a cartoonist eh?' said Maurice the optician, 'Just what we need!'

Oh goody thought I, as I envisaged working for some lucrative glossy optician's trade rag. But no, that was not the case. It appeared that Maurice the optician was a spare-time leftie who worked with a group of similar-minded activists, producing a small publication with very radical tendencies. 'We have meetings every month', Maurice the optician continued. 'Do come along. I'm sure you will be able to help us.' As I had just moved into the area and was feeling a little isolated, I agreed to come along, if only to meet some new people. 'We need some cartoons to jolly our magazine up a bit,' Maurice the optician remarked on parting. So, as promised the following week I attended the meeting, held in an upstairs room, next to the town hall. I was greeted by several baggy trousered revolutionaries and their Molls, straight from Central Casting. Ten people in all, of which it transpired, *eight* were the collective 'editor' of this radical magazine, known to very few as CRAB. I was shown a copy of the magazine, (the one needing jollificating). It was explained that CRAB was produced each month with the benefit of a true Democratic Ideal.

'This is Fred, he writes the editorial. This is Monica, she subedits the editorial. This is Gilbert he proof-reads the editorial. This is Eric he re-writes the editorial... and this is Jo. She organised our 'Sack Thatcher The Milk Snatcher' protest march last year, and she was eight months pregnant at the time'. I didn't enquire as to whether her pregnancy was the outcome of a true Democratic Editorial Ideal.

So I sat in the corner of the room for the rest of the evening and listened to heated polemic. The magazine got scant attention until, right at the end, a decision was taken to discuss the next issue. A motion was then passed to the effect that in future, all editorial meetings would discuss the magazine. This all seemed reasonable to me, a mere newcomer to radical thought. And then I was unanimously voted in as paste-up, layout and general magazine

artist. The ensemble was visibly relieved, when I unconditionally accepted the post, not so much because of my undoubted skill at magazine work but more because none of the collective assembled political geniuses considered the task of layout and paste up a fitting job for the architects of the New Britain. I took a copy of CRAB magazine home with me to study.

What an utter shambles it was. Home-duplicated on a knackered litho machine. Over and under inked on the same page. Printthrough, smudges, typos, the lot! This poor excuse for a magazine was actually on sale at five pence. Not surprisingly, sales were very low. About two hundred copies were printed, half distributed to a local factory and the rest found their sorry way into a few shops, or hand-distributed in the shopping precinct. Sales were falling every month. It now dawned on me that I had been roped in to jazz up the magazine's pitiful appearance in the wild hope that it would improve its chances in the market place. However, it was never apparent to our motley collection of Trotskyests, Maoists, Commies and Co-operatives that it was the *message* not the medium that was anathema to the citizens of Chelmsford town. However, I was eager to please, full of plans, roughs, typefaces, gate-folds and cartoons.

At the next editorial meeting all heads, if not hearts, turned in my direction. I proceeded to display my fresh and gleaming Letraset-ed proof copy of the new, redder than red CRAB. It proved a success and I started as paste-up artist that very night. The plates had been booked at a local printer for the following day, but you can't impress the need for a deadline on a den of dreamers and at CRAB, I had eight to deal with.

The evening chugged on and still nothing had arrived at my corner. Across the room a woman sat typing the various offerings for me to paste up, but no sooner had she finished one sheet, it was then pounced upon by one of the 'editors' and 'edited' and then another 'editor' 'edited' the 'edits' and so on around the room. This absurd situation persisted until, in desperation, I grabbed at the pages as they left the typewriter in order to get anything at all stuck down. Once it took three hours to decide whether a 'Coming Events' item should be included. By the time they had decided, no

doubt the event had gone.

I had reserved the back page of the magazine for a Dicky Howett cartoon. My cartoon was not specifically political. No Capitalist in a top hat and tails bashing a dungaree-clad loon on the bonce with a sack of South African gold. My cartoon (and others in the magazine) were social comments targeting the failings of petty officialdom and the like. I thought that the general readership would appreciate the injection of local flavour, but our gang of eight had other ideas.

After every issue of CRAB, the public were invited to attend a meeting with the express purpose of criticising the issue and offering suggestions. Only the editors and their friends ever seemed to turn up, but the exercise was never considered pointless. After a few praises and grumbles about minor points, my layout was generally approved until an unidentified individual stood up and wanted to know why the Howett cartoons were funny. He was not seeking an intellectual discourse on humour, he was just puzzled that humour should be used so freely in a political journal. 'I don't like all this funny stuff' he concluded. I sat stunned. Where am I? thought I. Then one of the editors, a snivelling gnome of an individual I had never really taken to, suddenly agreed with the questioner. He too had disliked my cartoons but had kept quiet for the sake of unity. And after all the hours I had spent sticking down their juvenile rantings! Then the rest of the ungrateful mob joined in and condemned me as a revisionist, whatever that was. It got all quite hectic.

I was understandably mortified at this incredible outburst, being quite unused to such displays of hostility and criticism. I seriously considered the possibility that there was something wrong with me. I hadn't known at the time that this kind of brain bashing was a regular feature of these 'readers meetings', all designed to deflate the ego and root out a cult of personality. My cartoons apparently had too much ego (*i.e.* 'me') in them. But I didn't understand this at the time and got all huffy and left. I was waylaid at the door by one sympathetic editor who explained this 'ego' business and tried to persuade me to return. But it was obvious that I was not suited to the cause. In fact, I could never have abided or accepted the

strictures of such a witless bunch, who so misunderstood the criteria of humour or were so negligent of the desires of the public they so desperately wanted to convert. The committee had wanted me to jolly their magazine up but in the end they proved they couldn't decide on anything, apart for discontinuing the magazine that is.

Ever the glutton for punishment, a year or two later, I teamed with journalist chum Jo Gable and we became briefly 'non-political' press barons. We devised and published a local newspaper called *The Chelmsford Independent*, a sort of regional consumer guide featuring *exposé* and general tattle. Naturally, this was not welcomed with open arms by local businesses. Our feature articles tended to criticise various pubs (sample text: '*The Running Mare's toilets had Running Mould*'), plus price comparisons at local supermarkets and the low down on, for example, bad dentists or council planning follies *etc*. Our 'hit list' was naively endless. But to our surprise, our first issue sold out! At least we thought it had. Unfortunately it was not to be. It transpired we had sold hardly any copies, due mainly to our faithless local 'distributor' neglecting to distribute copies. A big pile of issue number one was found in his warehouse hiding under a big box. The main local newspaper (or so we believed) had exerted a little pressure. Live and learn. Ho-hum.

Around that time, the town of Chelmsford decided to hold an Arts Festival and local artists were invited to apply for space to display their works. The 'space' was the railings down by the River Chelmer' (a fetid stream which runs sluggishly through the town centre). In eager anticipation, I pinned up my stuff and awaited sales. Well, let's face it who had ever heard of me? No sales all day, until at last, my next door neighbour took pity and bought a cartoon. Needn't have bothered really.

Chelmsford. Flogging cartoons on the railings in 1970s beard.

Newspaper baron.

SHE Magazine, December 1973.

CHAPTER 10

Supermum of Chelmsditch

On the Dec 1ˢᵗ 1977 along came *Supermum*. This full-page, twelve-frame strip was featured in IPC's *Whoopee!* comic and it was my very first attempt drawing for the kiddies humour market. At the time, Bob Paynter was the editor and it is to him I owe my 'break'. Bob confessed later, in his cups, that he thought I was going to be one of the best children's cartoonists in the UK. Unfortunately, prophecy wasn't one of Bob's stronger points.

Supermum, or Margie Mussels to give her real name, was a sort of high-speed super heroic Old Mother Riley. Supermum resided in a town called 'Chelmsditch'. I am nothing if not original because her environment closely resembled my home town of Chelmsford. She had a son called Terry and a monosyllabic husband who was seen usually slumped in an armchair uttering 'Umms', 'Ooohs' and the occasional 'YIKE!' when Supermum shifted his chair suddenly or sneezed.

The *Supermum* strip had originally been offered to a well-known singles cartoonist called SAX (Vic Sarkans). He had attempted a treatment but felt unable to develop it further for publication. Apparently he couldn't instil the characters with the necessary whoosh, zip and blam!, the vibrancy of kids cartoons.

I was not at all confident when the strip was offered to me. I had never undertaken a weekly full-page cartoon strip before, but at least my single cartoons showed a degree of movement which is, I suppose, why the editor chose me. I did quite well.

Within a year *Supermum* had gained so much popularity (via votes submitted) that it was decided to 'run a competition'. Enter the great 'Win-a-T-shirt' contest. The winnable T-shirts were hand-painted (special iron-on stuff) by me. I did ten and was paid £100. My daughter Lucy and I were photographed for publicity purposes at IPC wearing a selection of these T-Shirts and in a very short time, the editorial staff waded through over 1000 eager entries, which, I was told, was something of a record.

To win a T-shirt the kids had to draw their own versions of *Supermum* and the best submissions won. I saw some of these pictures and they were quite illuminating and touching. Several kids had, alarmingly, copied my style exactly, even down to my signature! Kids miss nothing, but nothing. Hector the Worm joined in quite soon after. I began adding him to the page as a sort of invertebrate Greek Chorus. One example had him dressed in dark glasses and a pastry case. 'I'm a mince-spy' he shrieked. Once, I drew a hole in the ground with a small notice which read, 'the worm's on holiday'. As a variation I would sometimes incorporate Hector in the design of one of the panels. He was perhaps, shaped like a cloud, a finger, or a dog's tail (nothing risqué of course). The readers then had to hunt for him, with the answer revealed in the letters page. Very useful this, as it enabled me to discover where I hid the bloody thing. I drew the strip two months on advance and I couldn't usually remember where I had hidden the worm. Kids, naturally, found him instantly!

I actually took *Supermum* on holiday. In those days we took three weeks family vacation on the small Channel Island of Alderney. So yes okay, I was getting a bit bored by the end of it. One year I carted my pens and inks with me. I had the scripts so I just whiled the evenings away and completed some artwork. Dedication or what? I even did a cartoon or two for the *Alderney Newspaper* which is about as small scale as you can get. Readership in the handfuls. Back from holidays, I was on a roll. My 'comic' draw-

Supermum, 1/1/77.

Dicky and Lucy, Supermum *T-shirts, 1978.*

ing style was unconventional (*i.e.* not based on the 1930s pattern) but I would be the first to admit that the style I adopted was not particularly appealing.

However, I felt I was improving all the time. Incidentally, all the strip's lettering was done in-house. All I had to do was leave sufficient spaces for the text. This was okay by me because my graphic skills had the proficiency of a backward 11-year-old. Fellow cartoonist and Supermum scriptwriter Roy Davis once criticised me for not being able to draw a convincing cartoon gorilla. He was absolutely justified because my simian attempt looked curiously like a hairy Benny Hill. Roy used to submit his *Supermum* scripts in the form of a full-page rough with all the panels sketched out. I could have just copied the lot, he was that good.

CHAPTER 11

A Guardian Angle and BBC East

Concurrent to drawing dodgy cartoon apes and disappearing worms, I was producing many highly specialised single cartoons for several bottom-of-the-pile, but top-of-the-shelf publications with titles such as *Sexy Laffs* and *Ribald Rudies*. No prizes for guessing the subject matter. I became quite adept at one-frame 'funny' smut, sometimes actually featuring bottoms and piles. I was churning out the stuff, and selling it at a phenomenal rate (a phenomenal rate, incidentally, that worked out at one pound per cartoon). Not riches untold to be sure, but all this proved to be an open drain into which I remorselessly tipped my wit. My cartoons covered the entire spectrum of sexuality (this was in the pre-PC days before certain themes were shunned or frowned upon). My dirty work was in great demand and I soon moved upmarket to *Men Only*, *Knave*, *Club International*, *Mayfair* and *Penthouse*. At one stroke I jumped from a one pound rate to a forty pound rate per cartoon, many drawn in full colour too.

During that period (1975) I became a member of the National Union Of Journalists (Funny Chapel Chelmsford branch) and was pushing for, believe it or not, a closed shop for all us pro cartoonists (CRAB had a lot to answer for). During one of our intermina-

ble NUJ meetings I was approached by journalist Anna Coote and in the course of our chat, Coote mooted a theme for an article she was considering for the *Guardian* newspaper. Something along the lines of man's sexual expression in an increasingly dehumanising society... or how sexist sex cartoonists earn a living (I hasten to add Ms Coote did not find me particularly sexist, nor indeed sexy for that matter). The *Guardian* liked the proposal and the article was duly published in the *Guardian* Women's page.

When it finally appeared, Coote's article, although entertaining and erudite, proved innocuous and rather inconclusive. Covering themes such as Donald McGill and naughty seaside postcards, later it described me as 'a mild and pleasant young man' an epithet more appropriate for a brand of milk stout than a highly talented cartoonist! The article as published, and my comments, seemed rather at odds as to what I remember saying. I recalled that Ms Coote and I spent a relaxing afternoon at my Chelmsford abode, covering many aspects of the cartoon trade and my aspirations within it. Okay, so I might have embellished things a bit. Not exactly *lying* but to be honest, most of it was quite near the truth. In the event and in glaring newsprint, I presented myself for all the world to see as an opinionated pillock. Thus I vowed in future to purport myself with all due caution and veracity. I didn't have long to wait for my resolution to be put to the test.

The day after Anna Coote's article appeared, I received a phone call from an assistant at the production office of BBC television's *Look East* which was (and still is) an Eastern regional programme transmitted early evenings from that fine city of Norwich. The assistant said that they had read Ms Coote's little item and as Chelmsford was just about within the East Anglian boundaries, I qualified for an appearance on the show. I agreed instantly, neglecting altogether to remember my vow of veracity. It seemed like another golden opportunity to make things up and this time on TV! The assistant said they would arrange to send a film crew the following week. The crew arrived at the appointed day but they were very late. I had planned to take them over to my allotment with me 'digging' around for ideas, a sort of visual pun. But it was now too dark and so, to make the best of it, we were all crammed

into my office. The director was quite scruffy looking and he wore a creased suit and a puzzled air. He explained they had just come from filming haddock at Harwich and were not quite sure why they were here. 'I got this call on my radio car phone, see. They said come down here. What do you suggest we do?' queried the director.

Oh dear, wrong question. So there they were, a full BBC crew, Director, Cameraman, Lighting Engineer, Sound Engineer and a woman interviewer, Australian if I recall, all waiting for me to invent something. I suggested rude cartoons, but that was quite out of the question, pre-watershed and all that. Thus we agreed to concoct a sort of local 'Look at Life', or 'How a Cartoonist Works In His Home With His Family There To Support Him'. A riveting theme to be sure.

Then we set about planning a totally scripted, spontaneous interview. The Aussie lady interviewer seemed in a bit of a dream and she spent most of the prep time staring fixedly at my crotch (my flared trousers *were* extremely tight in those far off days). Eventually we finalised some questions and ripostes with a selection of my cartoons pinned to the wall to use as cutaways. All I had to do was remember a few key words during the interview so that later, the film editor could splice in a shot of the relevant cartoon. Things started smoothly enough. I sketched a cartoon 'on camera' explaining to the viewing thousands what I was doing and then adding the punch line at the end. To the manner born, thought I. Then things started going wrong. I began forgetting the script and for some inexplicable reason my mind wandered to the camera with all that expensive Eastman colour film stock racing through the gate at 25 frames per second. Hurry, hurry, say anything! And than I heard myself spouting utter cobblers about how my favourite cartoonist was Carl Giles (not) and how I wanted to be a political cartoonist (not) and how my three year old daughter Lucy gave me lots of ideas for cartoons (never). Magic words to the director, because that meant now a link to the 'family situation' and the camera was moved to my living room with my cute offspring grizzling in the corner. Lucy steadfastly refused to perform on camera. No amount of cajoling made any difference. Kids have a nose for bullshitters.

Eventually the director announced a 'wrap'. He seemed pleased with everything. 'Ron got some nice shots of your hand drawing,' he said. 'We can easily cut all this down to six minutes.' I expressed disbelief. I mean, to start with, one of sentences was at least six minutes long and then there was all that stuff with my pens and inks and sharpening pencils not to mention my Eagle comic collection. But no, things were just fine and dandy. 'We'll let you know when it's transmitted,' the director said as they left, 'they may even pay.' Actually, I had been meaning to ask them to cough up for the electricity they used (the lamps were very bright) but thought better of it. I was hoping for a repeat performance and didn't want to spoil my chances.

Two weeks later, when the interview was transmitted, it shone as a masterpiece of artifice. My snivelling brat was transformed into a golden commercial for washing-up liquid, sitting attentively at my wife's side and giggling as her famous daddy read her a comic. I remember that bit, that was after I dragged her into the bathroom and threatened to dismember her rag doll. Her film giggles were probably stifled hysteria. But the greatest revelation was of 'Dicky Howett TV Star and his voice'. Gone was my imagined deep masculine well-modulated bass. Instead, erupting from the TV set was a curious whiny chirruping tone plus lots of sniffing. But nobody else seemed aware of this and my performance was praised by friends and for a short time, neighbours pointed at me in the street. I had recorded my performance on an audio tape and clicked a few snaps off the screen (the days before VHS video) but as with most transmitted stuff, my specific TV appearance had vanished into the cosmos, never to be viewed again... Or had it?

Let us scroll forward eighteen-or-so years. By the 1990s I was supplementing my cartoon work by writing media-related articles for several niche publications (*What Video, Camcorder User, Complete CD* and so on). I was commissioned by one to write a series about film and TV archiving. This lead me to the East Anglia Film Archive, established in 1976 and based at the University Of East Anglia near Norwich. Curator of the archive was David Cleveland whom, incidentally, I had worked at the BBC's Ealing Studios projection department way back in 1964. David was keen

to publicise the archive which, at the time, housed over 14,000 items, preserved on all film gauges, 8mm, Super 8, 9.5mm, 16mm, 28mm and 35mm. Video tape was stored in a special 'magnetic free' vault. During our interview David told me that he was in the process of acquiring and storing all of the film footage from BBC East with the eventual purpose of preserving the entire regional back catalogue. Perhaps then my 1975 *Look East* 16mm colour interview was saved and could I see it? Sorry no, BBC East had junked everything prior to 1976. It transpired that when the *Look East* 'Film Library' shelf got filled, they would chuck out the oldest cans to make room for new items. Brilliant scheme. Thanks, BBC.

CHAPTER 12

A Club for Cartoonists

Drawing or devising cartoons all day was, for me, a solitary business. A little light relief needed perhaps? The Cartoonists Club Of Great Britain (which, I believe still exists, the Club not Great Britain. Although that might be in some future no doubt). Anyway, back to the past. I joined the Club in the early 1970s and looked forward each month to the regular monthly meetings held in a pub just off Shoe Lane. The pub was named The Cartoonist and several of us would spend a convivial evening trying to match our *nom de plumes* with our actual names and visages. I always signed myself as 'Dicky Howett' but some cartoonists hid behind oddities such as 'Naylor' (James Gubb) 'Quanda' (Frank Holmes) or 'Belespot' (Allen King). If those are unfamiliar, grander figures sometimes graced the pub, Bill Tidy, Terry Parkes (Larry), Frank Dickens, John Burns, Kipper Williams, even the great Frank Hampson (although as a Club member he never, to my knowledge, visited). It was pleasure also to meet Denis Gifford, that pre-eminent collector and font of all things Comic. He always gave me encouragement, and indeed he commissioned me to draw a full page strip cartoon for his wonderful *Ally Sloper* magazine (the final issue as it transpired). Denis was working on a popular Thames TV show called

Quick On The Draw (1974-1979) which featured Bob Monkhouse and Bill Tidy being witty with a pen, plus a bunch of guest 'comedians' who couldn't draw a line and weren't much funnier. Denis tried several times to get me on the show, but as luck would have it, when it looked as if I might at last have been invited, the programme got canned.

I mentioned the signing of names to cartoons. On one occasion I ducked out of being Dicky Howett and became instead, 'Dave Richards', this for an exemplar gay monthly magazine called *Jeremy* (1969) billed as 'The Magazine For Modern Young Men'. The magazine had been devised and commissioned by a personable fashion photographer called Peter Marriott. He had had the inspiration for a timely glossy men's magazine and had somehow considered yours truly as suitable for the post of Art Editor, Paste Up Artist, General Illustrator and Cartoonist. Thus, I set about designing themes and styles, aided and abetted by my bemused wife Margaret and liberal quantities of Letraset. Along the way, I proposed a humorous strip entitled *James Blond: The Randy Dandy With The Handy Pandy*. This strip contained extremely sophisticated repartee which included James Blond announcing that he 'got where he was by starting at the 'bottom''.

I roped in chum Christopher Priest as 'Features Director: Richard Harrington' and Chris provided some excellent short story and other text material. The 48-page magazine (which looked very classy, if I say so myself, I even thought up the magazine's name) had film reviews, cooking, fiction, cartoons, a horoscope called 'Heavenly Bodies' and many fashion images. Peter Marriott advertised this magazine (in *Private Eye* amongst others) on the basis of subscription, or direct sale only. It was never intended as WH Smith top-shelf material. Soon, the postal orders (six shillings a copy) came flooding in.

What killed the magazine (after one issue) was twofold. Remember, the Sexual Offences Act had only been on the statute books for two years, and (although it was still the Swinging Sixties, just), the moral minority 'Festival Of Light' brigade could have found any old excuse to prosecute. Why? Well it was never put to the test, (because Peter quickly withdrew the magazine from

Ally Sloper.

sale), but perhaps an object of complaint could have been of a nudist image, (quite innocuous), showing a full-frontal teenage boy on a beach? And another of a teenaged boy in y-fronts (fashion section). However, as far as I was concerned, the other, more pertinent reason for ditching the magazine was that I never got paid my full fee of £200. Nuff said.

After that small stumble, my cartoon career progressed. Apart from dear old *Supermum*, I drew further feature strips for 'in house' magazines including for a firm of risk assessors. So what, you may well ask, is funny about risk assessment? Very little, to be honest and even less for another trade magazine aimed at pharmacists, where themes tackling pile pills or condoms need extremely careful handing to avoid descending into the lewd. Other interesting work arrived including designing a brochure for expectant mothers, and another for microwave ovens ('Instant Kitchens'. Yet another unpaid account, still awaiting the £25, mate!).

And then the BBC entered again. In all honesty the corporation never really left my life and hasn't yet. During the 1970s I had acquired an agent. Her name was Janet Freer and occasionally she found unusual assignments for me. Although primarily a literary agent, I believe she took me on as a novelty side-line. On one occasion, she asked me to attend a recording at Lime Grove studio G. Nothing spectacular, just a BBC training exercise for a tyro TV director called Martin Everard. The director, as part of his training remit, had to mount a 'real' programme. His idea was called *7 Up* which was an early venture into breakfast TV. This was way before actual breakfast television appeared to delight us all. I had two spots on the show where I sat at my easel and drew some topical cartoons. Of my performance I have no real memory apart from, during rehearsal, hearing the director screaming (a cameraman's headset was turned up full) to get me to 'start his bloody scene'. I had misheard my cue and had waited in silence whilst the camera homed in. I should have been talking away when the camera homed in. No praise for me there then. The director did later confess he had tried to get Bill Tidy to take part but got me instead.

Cartoonists at Butlins.

CHAPTER 13

Enter the Mighty Quinn

I first encountered a certain individual called Quinn at a convention for comic artists and writers. This was Strips 78 held at the Y hotel, just off Tottenham Court Road in London. The convention was one of Denis Gifford's little enterprises, held for no discernible reason and the place was full of cartoonists and guests. During a fag break I was approached by a diffident and unassuming character. He announced himself as being Tim Quinn and professed to be an avid fan of my work. He said also that he wrote scripts for D.C. Thomson and in particular *Dennis the Menace*. We soon got into a discussion about, mainly the poor state of British comics (in hindsight, a continuing moan of ours). I suggested to Tim (more to cheer him up really) that he submit a few scripts for my strip Supermum and this he duly did. I really thought no more of it. To be honest, I didn't fancy the idea of *Supermum* becoming another D.C. Dennis. But my doubts proved unfounded, because Tim's scripts (once they had been filtered through editor, Bob Paynter) were a breath of fresh air, full of originality and invention and importantly, funny! At last the 1930s had been left behind! It was now time to cook with gas!

Later, Tim had an idea for a feature entitled *The Gold Rush*.

This strip, (cunningly designed to last forever) had two loony lads rushing around the entire globe competing and searching for an inheritance. We both took the idea to Bob Paynter, but as we all drifted up in the lift at IPC's formidable Kings Reach Tower HQ, Tim announced suddenly to Bob and myself that 'Tim and Dicky' had won an American Best Cartoon Team Of The Year contest. Perhaps Tim was feeling particularly insecure at the time, but I just nodded and concurred at this Quinn fiction and hastily changed the subject before the lift doors opened. This fanciful 'award' was never ever mentioned again.

Supermum charged on until the end of 1981 when, for reasons unknown, it was peremptorily cancelled. The strip itself was highly popular and throughout its run, appeared in many Summer Specials and even graced the front cover of *Whoopee Comic* several times. *The Gold Rush* strip had finished a year earlier and now I was left with no IPC comic work at all. Tim and I pushed a few ideas but nothing appealed. I did have the inkling of a suspicion that my adult cartoon work was somehow influencing the editors and their decisions to dump me. But hey ho, and onward. Tim had suggested earlier that we contact a strange little outfit in Kentish Town called Marvel Comics and thus when one door closes... about ten others open.

CHAPTER 14

The Marvellous Marvel Years

Ten. I think that was about the number of weekly Marvel maga-zines that Tim and myself had our cartoons published in. It seems barely credible, but back at the beginning of the 1980s, Marvel UK (Or MUK as it was known, affectionately) was out to conquer the UK specialist comic magazine market. Reprints of *Spider-man*, *The Incredible Hulk*, or *The Mighty Thor* were cleverly re-pack-aged as the *Marvel Super Hero* series, attractive and competitively priced.

Tim's initial jolly Marvel idea was called *I Was Adolf's Double*. As the title suggests, it was a rollicking World War Two adventure featuring a bunch of fun-loving Nazis and an innocent Ramsgate gardener called Winston S. Quaill, who was Hitler's eponymous double. There was bit of initial trouble with Winston's surname. Tim had wanted to call him 'Cohen', but editor Paul Neary scrubbed that and replaced it with 'Quaill', which made no sense to us. We didn't argue, being Marvel new boys. We were just relived to have found a seemingly receptive market for our work.

I spent many delightful hours sketching the world's pre-eminent genocidal maniacs in a comical, but at the same time, deeply un-flattering light. I had noticed in the old newsreels that Goebbels

was a cripple who walked like a wonky pigeon so I made him a dwarf and gave him great pointy feet. Hermann Goering was depicted as a loud-mouthed fat git and Lord HawHaw, the traitorous radio correspondent was portrayed as a Rolls Royce-riding, top hatted, monacled upper class tit, dontcha know.

The series ran for 15 weeks in *Forces In Combat* and it was only recently that I discovered a small and, in retrospect, a very insensitive joke that I had innocently inserted into one of the frames. As was my practice, I habitually embellished Tim's scripts with visual puns. Part 12 of the series began with a 'Berlin High Strasse' scene and on a vacant lot, 'The Reichstag Nazi Gang Hut'. On the wall next to the hut was a poster which read 'Non Aryans Welcome at Billy Belsen's Holiday Camp'.

A few years later the entire 15 week run of *Adolf* was reprinted in our one-off Summer Special Marvel publication, *Channel 33⅓ The Children's Comic TV Station*. My holocaust holiday camp reference was never commented upon. What *did* get up somebody's nose was all the references to glue sniffing, prostitution and fornication. An irate parent had imagined seeing all this in our Special, enough to complain loudly to the editors and threaten prosecution. Copies of the magazine were sent to the Metropolitan police, but nothing ever came of it. Tim and myself were thus fortunately spared the prospect of having to while away our 'time' devising humorous prison news sheets for fellow inmates.

Tim's next jolly idea was a three-frame strip cartoon satirising all of Marvel's superheroes. We called the strip *Earth 33⅓*. My inspiration and model for the format was a similar series running in the USA by a cartoonist called Fred Hembeck. In my arrogance, I thought I could do much better. In all honesty I really struggled to characterise the Marvel Super Heroes. Some of my drawings of the Marvel Super lads and lassies were almost recognisable. These strips, which we churned out (daily it seemed), appeared across the entire Marvel weekly comic range. I was not then (or now) in any way a Marvel Super Hero fan, nor indeed a comic book reader. I had no real understanding what or whom I was drawing, but like a true professional I just blagged my way through and stuck it out, if only for the money.

I Was Adolf's Double: Billy Belsen.

Earth 33⅓.

Queen Thatcher and the Ayatollah Doll.

Hulk Hooligan Party.

Which brings us to *Jet Lagg: The Fastest Slowcoach In The Galaxy*. This was our next feature strip for Marvel and Tim and I had high hopes for this one. Jet Lagg's first adventure had him, and sidekick, the curiously named *Spunky*, battling with a clockwork Ayatollah doll and a giant Margaret Thatcher. This, to us, seemed a reasonable collection of villains (after all it was the innocent 1980s with all those awful murderous reprisals very much in the future) but no, Mr Editor hit heads and we had to change things. Any reference to an Ayatollah got scrubbed and Thatcher became *Queen Kong*. Upon publication, the observant might have noticed some hastily drawn hair on Thatcher's face but otherwise she still looked very much like the old hand-bagging milk-snatcher we all knew and loved.

But nevertheless, undaunted by incomprehensible editorial directives, we plugged away at Marvel UK and offered even more humorous feature strips. *The Fairly Amazing Spider Hound* (who attained his powers by being bitten by a radioactive flea) and *The Fantastic 400* which a gleeful Tim negligently foisted on me. This meant I now had to draw at least 400 new characters, usually in the same frame, and I did! Even later, for an American child's magazine he adapted *The Fantastic 400* and transformed it into *The Fitness 500*! Thanks Tim.

Another prize character was *Hulk The Menace*, an exquisite combination of Dennis the Menace and The Incredible Hulk. Tim imbued *Hulk The Menace* with all the attributes he had been denied when scripting the vapid D.C. Thomson *Dennis*. This new improved Hulk-type Dennis now ate copious quantities of baked beans and farted for all he was worth. That was all okay. Nothing wrong with a good honest honk. What was *not* okay was the depiction of the Hulk Hooligan Party. Politics again, so they had to be careful I suppose. *Hulk The Menace* was standing as his own Hooligan candidate, but this was way too much for Marvel. It was election year in the UK, and the editors decided that *H.T.M.* might influence voters with his decidedly loony tune views (nowadays we have UKIP for that). I drew up the three 'election' themed scripts, numbers 57, 58 and 59 and submitted the finished artwork, but those three were never published. I still have all the originals. Quite

a nice caricature of BBC interviewer Robin Day in there too. Oh, and a TV camera...

Tim and myself were quite a prolific team during the 1980s. Our combined efforts appeared in a multiplicity of magazines. One such was a strip aimed at video game fans (*TV Gamer*). We also approached regional posh county magazines such as *Essex Countryside*, who published our little pseudo local histories written by Tim, and bedecked with my apposite illustrations. We also contributed to a Fan Aid charity magazine, this about the time of the Geldof funfest at Wembley. But, as we now considered ourselves to be a top flight cartooning team, we became less charitable towards 'bloody editors', who were certainly getting under our collective skins. So we thought: here's an idea, let's be our *own* editors! Simps.

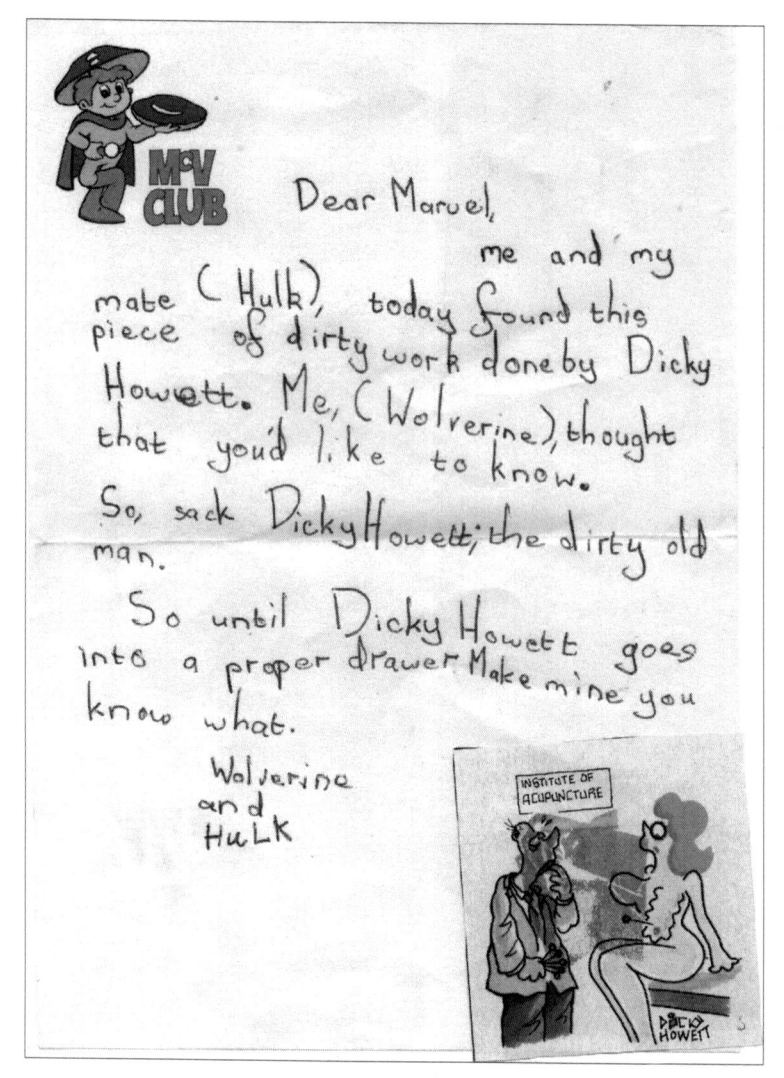

Dear Marvel,

me and my mate (Hulk), today found this piece of dirty work done by Dicky Howett. Me, (Wolverine), thought that you'd like to know.

So, sack Dicky Howett; the dirty old man.

So until Dicky Howett goes into a proper drawer Make mine you know what.

Wolverine
and
HuLK

INSTITUTE OF ACUPUNCTURE

Fan mail.

85

CHAPTER 15

Zip Goes a Comic Dummy

It seemed a jolly good wheeze: Cut out the top bozo and edit to our own taste. A comic for the 1980s at last! It was apparent that I couldn't realistically draw the entire thing, and so I contacted a few of the top British comic artists to see if they would contribute artwork (free) for a dummy issue. The response was gratifying. I got swift replies from the cream including David Lloyd, Ed McHenry, Nick Baker, Nigel Edwards, Jim Barker and the peerless Ron Tiner. With the finished artwork in place, I assembled the dummy issue which we named *ZIP!* and began the usual soul-destroying process of hawking the wares. Unbeknownst to me, Tim had decided (upon advice) to create a 'news item press release'. One of *ZIP!*'s strips was entitled *The Devil Wants You* and a frame showed some skin heads (under the influence of 'The Devil') on the rampage and in another, a man was shown attempting to murder his wife. Simple, warm-hearted kids stuff you will agree. This dastardly product was picked up by, amongst others, lovely old ITN. (they 'fell' for the bogus news item). I was in London at the time delivering some artwork to *TV Gamer* magazine. Whilst in the office I made a phone call Tim, (a query or something). Tim suddenly informed me that ITN had just recorded an interview with him

'down the line' and it was to be broadcast on the ITN one o'clock news. What was all this all about then, I pondered.

Devil artwork by Ron Tiner.

As ITN's Wells Street studios were but a short stroll from the *TV Gamer* office, at noon, I ambled in and identified myself, asking if I could kindly watch the broadcast from the foyer? To whit I was whisked straight into the studio and plonked next to Leonard Parkin. 'You can do the interview' they told me.

So cue Leonard with me sitting clueless beside him, waiting to be asked questions about what, I didn't know exactly. I must have mumbled something reasonably comprehensible because soon, the interview was over and Leonard graciously thanked me. A nice man. Afterwards in the green room I met some more TV faces and showed them a few of my cartoons. Agreeable afternoon. Got paid thirty pounds too. A very brief fragment of VHS recording exists, (a friend suddenly recognised me) and he punched the record button, rather too late to catch much. But for all that careful media manipulation, our *ZIP!* comic sank before it had even started, never to see the light of day again. I still have all the wonderful dummy artwork.

After the absolute total failure to interest any print publisher, Tim and I reimagined and retitled *ZIP!* into *ARGH!*. For this we approached the various television companies to try and enthuse

Argh! Quinn and Howett: TV presenters.

them in a TV series about cartoons and comics featuring, naturally, Tim and Dicky as the writers and star presenters. I cobbled together a nice little illustrated *ARGH!* prospectus which we brandished around the various TV production offices. The initial spark was the imminent arrival of cable television. The 1980s had been a time of deregulation and Cable Laying was flavour of the decade. Tim had assumed that nascent cable TV companies would be crying out for material (not true at all) but we began big by approaching the national broadcasters, like Channel 4 and Granada and then reduced our expectations down to regional companies like TVS and Anglia.

Tim and I traipsed around the studios and at one a commissioning editor (for TVS) kept asking us continually *why* we wanted to present a TV show about comics. I had not the balls to reply, 'because I want to be fucking famous and earn lots of cash, chum!' Rejections didn't stop us. Give us an excuse and we would contact any old outlet that would have us. Later, our two cartoon books, the *Doctor Who Fun Book* and *It's Bigger On The Inside* set us off on a round of frenzied promotions: Liverpool, (Granada) Leeds, (YTV) Norwich, (Anglia TV). Local radio even, perhaps not the best medium to promote a purely visual product, but hey, we were in the spotlight again and did we love it!

Our first major television appearance was in 1980, when we convinced the mighty BBC that Quinn and Howett really ought to be on the small screen. Marvel UK had just produced a 'science fiction' magazine called *Future Tense* which included our latest cartoon offering *The Concise History of the Galaxy*, not a million miles from a sort of *Hitchhiker's Guide*. A notable feature in our history was that it didn't have a paranoid android but instead, a peripatetic talking toilet bowl. Perfect, we thought, for little Noel Edmonds and the shambling Saturday morning hit show, the *Multi-Coloured Swap Shop.*

Tim and I were duly invited to Television Centre to be assessed (I now realise) and to watch the programme from the gallery as it was transmitted. We seemed to pass some sort of BBC test because we were later booked to appear live on the 100th edition of *Swap Shop* which took place on the 1st November 1980 in the spacious

surroundings of (the now demolished studio) TC7. Tim, who had dragged along, for reasons still unclear, a young lady named Fiona Menzies, and I arrived at TVC at the appointed hour (9am) armed with our various bits of artwork. I had prepared these previously, several large, and not very accomplished, display strips concerning the programme. For example, the camera crew 13 was a running joke, plus a 'competition' cartoon and some prizes. We had no rehearsal as such, but were just shoved straight in to get on with it. The rigours of live TV.

Quinn and Howett on Swap Shop.

Positioning ourselves at a table in the 'Coffee Shop', we awaited the time to be introduced. On cue, Noel immediately launched into a question about 'the dire state of comics today'. Tim then started to argue the point and I had to interject by declaring that what we were trying to do was 'very different', and then asking for a bigger table to draw my pictures on. Not a very good start.

Things improved and during our next 'spot' and we managed

to mention Marvel's *Future Tense* magazine five times in five minutes. The morning raced by and all too soon it was over. We had met some nice people like the beautiful Jan Leeming plus Maggie Philbin and Seb Coe, for whom I drew an instant caricature (I was warned in advance by one of the young ladies who accompanied him that he was a bit sensitive about his nose). Seb had brought along his Moscow Olympics gold medal. I don't know what I was expecting to see, but the medal looked to me suspiciously like a large gold foil covered chocolate penny.

Quinn flogging the mag on Swap Shop.

Also on the show was dear old Matthew Waterhouse, the much maligned actor who was then portraying the character Adric in *Doctor Who*. Like star-struck, disingenuous groupies we copiously praised Matthew for his recent performance as the latest *Who* companion number whatever...

Swap Shop regularly ran competitions and Tim and I had a nice, frameable colour cartoon, specially drawn by me, as a prize. Also, we had other 'prizes', of which one of mine was a 1950 copy

of the BBC Handbook. Gee, how interesting *that* must have been for the average pre-teen viewer! After the show, I got into conversation with the programme's editor, Rosemary Gill. She was leafing through my 1950 BBC Handbook 'prize' and alighted on a picture of very well known female artiste. 'I could tell you some stories about her', said Rosemary. I was all ears but unfortunately Rosemary was interrupted at that juncture and I never got the dirt dished. All this social history just vanishing away. Poo! I don't know whether the BBC Archive has a recording of this 100th *Swap Shop* show. Probably, but I certainly do (on VHS). I would be willing to part with it, if requested, for a suitably large finder's fee.

Previous to our appearance on *Swap Shop*, Tim had alerted the editor of *Oh Boy* magazine, a ditzy publication for negligible intellects. The editor liked Tim's idea for a modern strip cartoon called *Livin' In The Eighties*. I then drew several pages of this stuff which was duly presented. However, the magazine's art director was totally unimpressed, criticising my drawings as all having 'pointed noses' But the art director was overruled editorially, and off we went. From that juncture my published strips got smaller and smaller on the page until the only comfortable way to view them was with a portable electron microscope. Obviously, a nasty case of Art Director's Revenge. The strip was canned after ten myopic weeks.

CHAPTER 16

Who's Writing a Bit on the Side?

Throughout the 1980s and the early 1990s our most enduring creation for Marvel was the *Doctor Who?* three-frame strip appearing in *Doctor Who Magazine*. This cartoon feature thrived under the changing editorships of notably Alan McKenzie, John Freeman, Gary Russell and Sheila Cranna. It helped very much that these editors had an abiding love for the *Doctor Who* programme and indeed, understood our take on the subject. It's generally acknowledged that our particular satirical cartoon slant on *Doctor Who* has never been equalled, spawning as it did many page features (*The Doctor Who History Tour, etc.*) and full colour strips in the various *Doctor Who* annuals. And then there was *The Doctor Who Fun Book* and *It's Bigger on the Inside*, one-off publications, both full of original strips and features. Lately, there has been the sell-out edition (and reprints) from Miwk Publishing entitled *It's Even Bigger on the Inside* which pulls together just about every Quinn and Howett *Doctor Who?* cartoon published, plus lots of private commissions never before seen in print, or indeed remembered by yours truly. However, now I think of it, I wonder what ever happened to the nude Peri cartoon I once sketched in a tipsy moment for a fan? The hunt is on!

Peri.

And so on the basis of our *Doctor Who* magazine cartoon work, Tim and I spent the late 1980s traipsing the Fan Convention trail. Some big, some small. Actually I quite enjoyed these conventions as it raised the opportunity to meet fans and also hob nob with the stars of the programme. Nice meeting Sophie Aldred, Louise Jameson and Debbie Watling. Also glamour film actress Caroline Monroe, whom I'd last spotted semi-clad in an edition of *Men Only* magazine. Not certain why naughty Caroline was at the convention. She may have been a fan or perhaps seeking to be a companion? Larger on the scale of convention guests was Colin Baker and the slightly smaller Sylvester McCoy. Our *Doctor Who Fun Book* had just been published and as a charity prize I asked the stars to sign a copy, although McCoy was rather grumpy about it. During these conventions, usually both Tim and myself sat at a corner desk where I drew little *Who* sketches (free of charge) and Tim practised his signature. Later, Tim devised scripted performances whereby we both made fools of ourselves by reading, on stage, short 'joke' episodes of *Doctor Who*. There exists, I believe,

Tall Tales (of Essex).

a video of one our 'acts'. This will doubtless return to haunt us. Indeed, on one notable occasion, at a London Comics Convention, we were actually booed off stage by various fan boy drunks.

In 1986, BBC Essex, a new local radio station, began transmitting from studios in Chelmsford. I sauntered in with an idea for a series of *Tall Tales (of Essex)*, designed as a monthly slice of topical nonsense, read on-air by myself. I proposed taking a local news item (a new shopping centre, a new sports pavilion, road repairs or lack of them *etc.*) and then weaving an unlikely 'history' all within the space of five minutes. A sort of aural cartoon strip. I wasn't a totally unknown entity to the corporation as at the time I was also the back-page cartoonist for the BBC's very own house journal *Ariel*, usually referred to by the wits at TV Centre as 'Pravda'. Incidentally, I had to be careful there. A cartoon of mine was praised for assisting in winning some sort of publishing prize for *Ariel*, but another cartoon I drew was dropped. This illustrated a piece about the recently established BBC Worldwide sales outfit. The cartoon depicted a spiv selling dodgy programmes captioned 'BBC WORLD *WIDE-BOY*'. Perhaps the editors didn't understand what a 'wide-boy' was... or indeed, dodgy programmes?

Dicky telling Tall Tales.

My *Tall Tales* scripts were written to incorporate music snatches interweaved as counterpoints (*The Sun Has Got His Hat On*, a few bars to indicate seasonably bad summer weather perhaps?). The first of my pre-recorded monthly *Tales* went out on Christmas Day 1986 and the second *Tale* went out on Boxing Day 1986, so from then on I was getting all behind.

I billed myself as the BBC Essex Alternative Historian, and although most of the listeners seemed unperturbed, or perhaps unaware, of my efforts to amuse, BBC Essex presenter Jules Bellerby absolutely hated my *Tall Tales*. Jules hosted the afternoon show and was obliged to run my offerings, usually without comment but occasionally with a snide aside. But I wasn't bothered, and in any case, a local publisher had bought a selection of my *Tall Tales* and had produced a nice little book, (still available on Amazon/eBay for about seventy pence) complete with my cartoon illustrations. When my book was launched, I was invited back onto Jules' show to unmercifully publicise it. Well I never.

But times they were a-changing. The Fleet Street revolution, spearheaded by the Murdoch press and anti-union legislation, facilitated mighty moves towards complete computerisation of the national press and magazines. One corollary was that page make-up with scissors and a pot of paste was now performed exclusively on a computer screen, so there was no need for 'spot' cartoons to fill awkward spaces in the pagination. Gradually, I was selling fewer 'singles' and many of my steady markets vanished, seemingly overnight. As mentioned earlier, I decided to reboot my writing and photography skills by aiming illustrated (photos and cartoons) articles at specific niche publications. My interests were radio, TV, cinema and audio so I planned a variety of features around those themes. One described my adventures with Compact Discs, (quite new back then) another about the local Air Cadets video club and still another about my attempts to 'home movie' recalcitrant pets, all under the guise of *How To Flippin' Well Do It*. I even, for a while, had my own back page 'last word' feature called *Back Tracks* in *Complete CD & Hi Fi Buyer* magazine. There I was, spinning the usual tall tales and plugging the merits of digital recording systems for the audiophiles. It's easy when you know abso-

lutely nothing about the subject.

For my media articles I was constantly searching for suitable material. I then discovered a quaint, privately-financed magazine called *405-Alive* (run as a hobby), by technical journalist Andrew Emmerson. Andy's magazine was a delicious mixture of old time TV and folk memories, harking back to the good old days of black and white television. I contributed to Andy's magazine with an increasing amount of written material, concentrating on interviews with television luminaries, including directors, video technicians and premier TV technology manufacturers such as Marconi's, EMI or Vintens.

I found great delight in meeting and talking to these television old-timers. One such was Daphne Shadwell, a name perhaps unfamiliar to most, but Daphne directed the original series of the frenetic TV pop music programme, *Ready Steady Go!*. She recalls, 'The title of the show actually came from me. Most TV directors started their programmes by counting down, "ten, nine, eight..." *etc*. I was different. I used to end the countdown with "ready, steady, GO!" That's how the show got its name. It was an in-joke'. Joke or not, *Ready Steady Go!* was innovative. Back in the 1960s, the current art form known as 'the pop promo' was then only a vague video notion. Spotty rock bands or solo singers could only promote their latest single live before unsympathetic cameras on 'square' programmes such as *Crackerjack!*, *Blue Peter* or *The Billy Cotton Band Show*.

Occasionally, a pop group might get full colour exposure on Rank's quirky and often sarcastic cinema series *Look at Life*, or be asked to make brief films for a short-lived system that used coin-operated movie jukeboxes which played songs and ran films, sometimes in sync.

Originally, Daphne Shadwell wasn't connected with *Ready Steady Go!*. As a staff director at the ITV programme contractor, Associated-Rediffusion she worked on anything that came up, mainly women's and children's shows. 'I directed the *Five O'Clock Club* which had quite a high pop music content. Muriel Young fronted that show and she also hosted a radio programme for Luxembourg called *The Green Room* which was a pop record show

with kids dancing and generally enjoying themselves. And then El-kan Allan, who was head of A-R's Light Entertainment, reported he'd seen the Dick Clark US pop show *American Bandstand* and wanted a similar show here. We combined Muriel's show with the Dick Clark programme format and that became *Ready Steady Go!*'

Daphne Shadwell was the youngest of four daughters of BBC Variety Orchestra conductor Charles Shadwell and began her life in broadcasting as a humble (they are always 'humble') BBC secretary. Says Daphne, 'That was in 1947 in the Near East and Latin American Service of the BBC which was situated at Aldenham House, Elstree. It wasn't the most exciting of jobs, but in those days we were grateful for anything. However, I constantly applied for other posts within the BBC. I finally went to 200 Oxford Street, where they produced *Forces Favourites*. That was fun. We used to watch the world go by from our office [the Peter Robinson building] high above Oxford Street.

'We used also to go swimming in our lunch hours at the nearby Marshall Street baths. We were reprimanded, however, for hanging our costumes out to dry on the balcony. Not very BBC!'

During 1947 Daphne Shadwell met her husband, TV director John P. Hamilton and they were married in 1954. The long courtship was out of necessity; they couldn't afford to marry on BBC wages! At the time, John P. was a BBC RPA (Recorded Programmes Assistant). He travelled the country with programmes such as *Down Your Way* and *Top of the Form*. Later, he added live spot effects on *The Goon Show*.

Back at Broadcasting House, Daphne Shadwell still applied for any BBC job going. It was while working in the BBC Duty room that she first entered television. 'In 1950 I became assistant to a producer called Pamela Brown,' says Daphne. 'Pamela Brown also used to write children's books, usually during BBC time which made her feel guilty. Anyway, I was sent down to Lime Grove; no training, never even been inside a studio before. I sat there open-mouthed watching a live cartoon show with Kenneth Connor voicing, *Simon the Simple Sardine*. Fascinating. I did everything on the production side, which is a good way to learn. Later, I was assistant to David Boisseau who directed *Muffin the Mule* up at Stu-

dio A, Alexandra Palace. Studio A had a production gallery that was entered by climbing a steep flight of open stairs. In the room directly below these stairs was the Emitron camera control equipment. I caused a sensation by climbing up the stairs wearing a very short skirt. From that moment I was a big hit with the engineers!'

Daphne Shadwell was soon directing cameras and artists. She became adept at calling shots, adding to her experience. In 1954, during a stint at Lime Grove, she met a *Whirligig* production assistant called Lloyd Williams who was surreptitiously recruiting BBC staff for the new commercial television station, Associated-Rediffusion. Daphne became Lloyd Williams' personal assistant at A-R with the promise of becoming a TV director herself when A-R started in 1955. Later, Daphne directed the Monty Python progenitor, *Do Not Adjust Your Set*, and also *Rainbow*, *Magpie*, *Splash*, *Hold The Front Page* and *The Sooty Show*.

Ready Steady Go! was produced live each Friday evening ('The weekend starts here!') from Studio 9 at A-R's Television House in Kingsway, London. The studio itself was small, (sixty-four foot by forty foot), and wedged-shaped with the scene doors orientated at the Bush House end of Kingsway. Daphne Shadwell, 'We crammed in about one hundred and twenty kids. We actually had a ticket waiting list of six thousand! With four large cameras and lights and everything, you can imagine it was a tight squeeze. But that's what made it so exciting. It was quite chaotic, but Keith Fordyce who introduced the show held everything together. It would all have fallen apart without him.'

An unusual feature of *Ready Steady Go!* was that no attempt was made to hide, on-screen, the TV cameras which could be observed amidst all the frantic pushing and shoving as they were manoeuvred across the studio floor. Daphne recalled, 'It didn't start that way, having cameras in shot. On one show in 1963 we had Jerry Lee Lewis who was a bit rude to me. He didn't arrive until the final rehearsal and when I went onto the floor to check on a few points he bellowed "Who is this woman?" We hadn't been introduced, you see. Come the live show, he was of course marvellous and during the finale he stood up and hammered away at his piano. All the cameras moved in, and to my horror I saw that in every

monitor, a camera was visible. I couldn't get away from them. It was a nightmare. So we just let them roll, and from then on if a camera got in shot, it stayed in shot!'

The camerawork on *Ready Steady Go!* was of a very high standard. The four studio cameras used were heavy and unwieldy. They were mounted on mechanical wheeled iron pedestals, which meant that cameramen had to heave at least 600lbs of equipment around the congested studio floor. Also, because the playback was extremely loud, the cameramen couldn't always hear the screamed instructions from the gallery, so they were relied on to offer shots. Some cameramen, like Bill Metcalf (who later became a BBC producer) had a natural gift and were always there when required, with an image correctly framed and interestingly shot. Other cameramen, perhaps used to leisurely discussion programmes or drama were not so responsive. However the studio cameras regularly rammed the audience. Daphne said, 'We always got injuries. It was the pan handles mainly that caught people in the back and on one occasion, a relative of Elkan Allan, a particularly obnoxious kid, was deliberately rammed.'

Ready Steady Go! made stars of Donovan, Billy Fury, Gene Pitney and 19-year-old Cathy McGowan, who chucked in a ten pound a week secretarial job to work on the show. 'Lovely girl, easy going,' recalls Daphne, 'not a brain in her head though. And the young American artists were also very nice to work with, very polite. Gene Pitney always joked that we tried every sort of entrance for him; outside in the scene dock, down stairs, up stairs, perhaps next he would be suspended from the lights! The studio was quite limited and the sets, quite basic, a few rostrums. Once we had Sonny and Cher and Cher brought in a dress she was going to wear for the transmission. The engineers wanted to test-light it and got Cher to hold the dress up in front of a camera. We actually forgot about her and later we noticed, what seemed like hours later, on the monitor, poor old Cher still standing patiently with her dress. We'd forgotten all about her, but she didn't complain or moan. Very professional'.

Daphne Shadwell has fond memories of her time as a TV director and especially the show, *Ready Steady Go!*. 'RSG was jolly hard

work. My favourite pop groups were The Hollies and the Troggs. I christened them "The Trollies", especially when we had a hole in the bookings. "See if the Trollies are available," I'd say. Some pop artists baffled me. I thought Jimi Hendrix most peculiar and one group, The Small Faces, held up rehearsals once when the lead singer unaccountably disappeared for a whole afternoon. It turned out he'd been at Wembley hospital getting a fix! I never thought of such things like pot or drugs, although they were around. I was so innocent, but it explained Jimi Hendrix. I suppose people thought I was a bit quaint, especially when I used to hand out lollipop sweets to the crew at the end of transmission.'

Another interview I did was with TV director, the late Michael Leeston-Smith. He was a pioneer of post-war BBC television production who worked on the first two *Quatermass* series and also directed a *Doctor Who* story: *The Myth Makers*, so this was of particular interest to me.

Michael Leeston-Smith was employed first in 1932 at Ealing Studios as an assistant sound recordist on some of the Gracie Fields films. After war service, Leeston-Smith worked for the BBC at Alexandra Palace, initially on the transmitter and subsequently as a junior studio lighting engineer working with renowned director Rudolph Cartier on *The Quatermass Experiment*.

This seminal 'horror' production was performed live from Studio A. The working area was only about fifty foot by twenty-eight foot and the insensitive pre-war Emitron cameras demanded vast amounts of light, putting great demands on the actors who suffered terribly with the heat (this being mid-summer). Because of the Emitron camera's shading problems (stray electrons within the tube which caused the picture to look patchy) a regular cry heard from the production gallery was 'chicken on camera' , referring to the shape of the fault. Leeston-Smith would then have to wheel five kilowatt spotlights to within a few feet of the actors in an attempt to iron out the 'chicken' and balance the picture. Sometimes things got so bad it was not unknown for the lighting level to be raised to ten kilowatt per actor!

Quatermass II (1955) was produced within the slightly more commodious surroundings of Studio G at Lime Grove. Working

now as a production assistant, Leeston-Smith would accompany Rudolph Cartier on location filming. Leeston-Smith recalls, "We were filming at Shell Haven refinery. The morning had gone well with lots of film in the can. All taken in full sunlight. Then the clouds blotted out the light and we stopped until it cleared. We positioned the camera to film a shot of Quatermass in a car entering the main gate of the refinery. Just as the sun came out Rudi called "stand by, turn them over!" Suddenly the siren at Shell Haven, went off and crowds of staff came wandering out. It was lunch time and they all sat in the sunshine around the main gate eating sandwiches. Rudi cried, at me "Mike get rid of them. Why did you let this happen? What's the use of an assistant who lets things like this occur?" Then the sun went in for good.'

In 1961, after six years on the technical side, Michael Leeston-Smith was given the job of director. The Head of Drama at the time was Michael Barry who gave Leeston-Smith his chance, leading to directing many episodes of the classic 1960s drama series *Z-Cars*. Leeston-Smith directed only one episode of *Doctor Who*. This was billed in the Radio Times as *Dr Who and the Trojan War*. 'John Wiles was a good producer,' says Leeston-Smith 'and it was great fun working with Max Adrian who played King Priam of Troy. Also Barrie Ingham who played Paris. Both marvellous actors.'

Although mainly studio-bound, this particular *Doctor Who* story demanded some outside filming, down at the often-used BBC location of Frensham Ponds. The BBC design department had constructed the necessary sets and the rest of 'Troy' was a model photographed using the 'Schufftan' process, a system devised by a German called Eugen Shufftan which involved an angled mirror with a section of the mirror's silver backing scraped off, then filming the reflected model combined with the live action beyond the hole. The wooden Trojan Horse was also a model and filmed similarly.

For a *Doctor Who Magazine* article, I tracked down a rather disgruntled retired BBC engineer called Joe Starie (described by colleagues as a 'legend in his own mind'). Joe worked at the BBC's Television Centre and in August 1963 was shift engineer when TC4 was booked for what was described as an 'experimental' session. The noted BBC designer Bernard Lodge was searching for a special

effect in order to create a title sequence for a new production called *Doctor Who*. It was decided to try something called 'positive feedback' or howlround. This effect is caused when electronic cameras 'see' their own output reflected back in a monitor and the image is repeated endlessly in a closed loop. These days that sort of effect can be digitally conjured, but back then it all had to be done optically and physically in the studio.

Joe Starie was called in and asked to set the position of an EMI 203 image orthicon camera and monitor. Says Joe, 'I began the electronic effect by keying the camera onto my pen-torch which I happened to have in my pocket. I waved the torch about for a few seconds and checked the monitor to see the results. The images started to show positive feedback. From then on I threw in everything I could offer. The most significant effects came when we reversed the scans in the camera which gave the now familiar swirling and twisting effect.'

The session lasted an hour and was recorded onto the old style 2-inch Quad videotape. Later, the best effects were chosen by the designer and mixed in with some previously filmed 'Doctor Who' title lettering. During our interview, Joe confessed that he had saved absolutely nothing from his days with the BBC, just his precious *Doctor Who* pen-torch that in retrospect, could have been said to have actually started it all.

Although I was now drawing and selling to fewer publications, one area that showed no signs of abating was the cartoon material I supplied to the men's top-shelf magazines. These included *Men Only*, *Penthouse*, *Mayfair*, *Razzle*, *Girl Illustrated* (yes, the magazine featuring a tumescent Dalek and a nude *Doctor Who* companion, the lovely Katy Manning), *Fiesta*, *Knave*, *Escort*, *The Journal Of Sex* (I wonder what that was all about) and Paul Raymond's *Club International*.

I had a colour three-frame strip running in *Club International* called *Movie Millie*. Millie, bless her heart, was a porn star who, every issue, was teamed with Big John, a prodigious chap who could 'extend' himself at least forty-five feet. Big John once had a cold and came to the studio with a very long, suspiciously red sausage-shaped 'scarf' wrapped around his neck many times. What fun we had.

Movie Millie.

I found that the editors for these adult magazines were by far the easiest to deal with. They seemed almost pathetically grateful for my cartoon work, but then I suppose there weren't many of us willing, or indeed able to draw the naughty stuff. Anyway, the pay rates were far above Fleet Street and so I just continued to churn it out and rake in the lolly. Years later in 2012, I was filming with Steve Coogan on *The Look of Love*, a Channel 4 biopic, based on the life of Paul Raymond. The location that day was in Berwick Street, Soho and opposite the pokey little *Club International* office where I used to deliver my *Movie Millie* cartoons.

Singular commissions sometimes arose. I was contracted to draw a daily three-frame cartoon strip for a Zambian newspaper. Now, to be honest, I was a little doubtful. A year or so previously, Tim and I had drawn a comic page for a Nigerian magazine which never paid us. The Zambian commission was different inasmuch that it was funded from a UK agency and the money was paid in advance. All I had to do was draw the life history of Zambia's president, Mr Kenneth Kaunda. Well why not?

The script was written by a freelance writer whose name escapes me, but the slight difference here for me was that the strip wasn't in any way comic, just a straight forward illustrated history of a real person. The apparent reason for the strip was that Kenneth Kaunda was standing for re-election and it was thought that a nice hagiography would help his chances. I didn't follow subsequent events in Zambia so I've no idea of the eventual outcome of the

election, but I was informed that although the commissioners liked my strip cartoon, which I drew in advance amounting to forty-two daily instalments, it was never actually published. Seemed a waste of the £1800 they paid me.

Kaunda unpublished artwork.

Back in the UK, in 1985 the Dundee publishers, DC Thompson had a prescient idea. Initially dubbed 'Project AM' it eventually emerged as *Celebrity* magazine, and it did exactly as described on the tin. The magazine was a precursor to all the *Hellos, Heats, OKs* and *Goodbyes* etc. that were later to grace the 'celebrity' publishing scene. So Tim and I submitted a strip called *G.E.T.* (apparently, a mild Liverpudlian insult) or *Great Enormous Twit*. This *G.E.T.* was a tale of other worlds and space ships with the eponymous hero Kevin Block zipping around the galaxy having spiffing adventures. DCT replied, (I have all the letters and extracts follow). 'Many thanks for submitting your *G.E.T.* space cartoons... also we envisage changing the title to *Twit in Space* which actually fits quite well with your own translation of Great Enormous Twit.' So Tim didn't get (as it were) away with *that* one!

Block Party, upstanding artwork.

The *Twit* commission proceeded and I completed colour artwork having first submitted pencil roughs prepared from Tim's scripts. These roughs were very important to the editors as it gave them ample opportunity to actually do a spot of editing. For example, editorial advice about Rough number 16: 'It concerns the "spitting" incidents, sorry not very Thomson-like. Not even "tasteful" spitting!' or '...not too keen on your "subliminal advertising ending"' or '...we once had a bit of bother with the *Blue Peter* producer so I'd appreciate it if you could water that association in episode 27.'

Intriguing. However, occasionally my roughs were returned having been tampered with, bits of dialogue or images altered, and commented upon thus '...thanks for roughs... episodes 40 to 45, no problems here apart from No. 42 which we'd like to drop.' No explanations were forthcoming here about any perceived problems with rough No. 42 but recently I found this rough and it's one of my favourites. It shows Kevin and Rabbie the Robot crashing through four cartoon 'frames', Plop! Plop! Plop! Plop! with a tag line about an emergency stop button. I cannot fathom the objec-

tion to this very nice (if I say so myself) bit of drawing and clever scripting. It actually encapsulated the Quinn and Howett cartoon humour approach and *raison d'etre*. Ho hum.

Twit in Space, *No. 42 rough.*

Eventually *Twit in Space* ended with issue 46 and it was replaced with some vapid humorous cartoon concoction more in keeping with editorial remits. Re-reading my correspondence with the editors of *Celebrity* magazine, I now get the distinct impression that they never *really* understood the humour of *Twit in Space*. I think they just encouraged us to be kind. So as a *Twit* character, Rabbie the Robot might have said, 'They may have laughed at Thomas Edison, but no' at the Glasgee Empire they didnae.' Nor apparently, at dear old Dundee DCT.

CHAPTER 17

On TV Again, Very Briefly

Tim's next spiffing wheeze was to reform and reinvent us both as television 'film critics'. Thus was born *Tim and Dicky's Take Two*. During Tim's sojourn in the United States (working for the *Saturday Evening Post Magazine*) he had come across a syndicated TV show hosted by a couple of film critics called Gene Siskel and Roger Ebert. Apparently this programme was extremely popular featuring as it did two eminent journalists, both with an encyclopaedic knowledge of Cinema. Tim had envisioned us doing likewise on British TV, disregarding the fact that we weren't in any way eminent journalists nor did we have the least part of an encyclopaedic knowledge of Cinema.

Tim arranged a meeting with the producers. This was for an ITV programme called *This Morning*, broadcast daily by Granada Television from the historic, and recently restored, Albert Dock complex in Liverpool. The thrust of our TV idea was in the form of a two handed criticism of current movies, with a 'one for' and 'one against' approach, giving 'thumbs up or down' to any given film. The idea seemed okay to me, if a little contrived. The nub of this exercise was the interaction between us as 'critics' and the resulting 'entertainment value' so derived. Thus *Tim and Dicky's Take Two*

aired on the 21st February 1989. It really should have been *Take One* because that was the first and last time it was ever seen.

What we did was this. We had two current movies lined up to 'criticise'. *Gorillas in the Mist* and *Fatal Attraction* (out on video in 1989). I professed to 'like' *Gorillas* and 'hate' *Fatal*. Tim, the opposite reaction. Previously we had obtained VHS copies of these films in order to review the subject matter and concoct our comments. *This Morning* then obtained broadcast quality extracts to transmit. We arrived at the studio, in good time for our rehearsal, and to cue up the film extracts. We had scripted everything and timed our performance to around eight minutes. Annoyingly, we never got our rehearsal, as something else intervened which needed the time. So, there we were, about to go out live on national TV, with a fully unrehearsed segment, trying desperately to read everything off autocue, something, I personally had never done in my life, (not at all difficult as it turned out). The programme started (hosted by singer Paul Jones and his wife, who were booked as holiday replacements for the usual presenters, Punch and Judy).

Tim and Dicky's Take Two.

Tim and I crept into our small 'cinema' set (popcorn, red plush seats, cigarette smoke, *etc.*) and awaited our cue to begin. During an ad break a frantic floor manager rushed over and asked us to cut our eight minutes down to five 'as we are overrunning!' We staggered through as best we could and finished more or less within the niggardly time allowed. Not our finest hour, I fear, nor indeed five minutes. We made the best of it, but I had a premonition that we were not really cut out to be TV stars and we would only have crash landed and been at odds with management at some point. Reviewing later the VHS off-air copy of our appearance, I noticed a sign hanging from the curtain behind us with read in large letters, 'Gentlemen's Cloakroom'. It seemed like a very unfair criticism of our masterly performances.

The artist in 1988.

With another prospective TV career shot down in smoke, we both, more in desperation I fear, had a try at the 'alternative' comics then in vogue (*Smut, Acne, Fizz, etc.*), but I personally had no

enthusiasm for this sort of arch 'amateur' publication. We placed a few strips including *Bloody Ages Ago* and *Doug & Del they Undertake Quite Well* (the less said about that the better!). To cap it all, our *Doctor Who?* strip had ground finally to a halt after around 224 issues, mainly because the *Doctor Who Magazine* publishers had sold the title to Panini and I suppose they wanted a different 'look'. So there it ended. Were we running out of ideas? No. Were we too expensive? Not really. The outcome, all change for the sake of it. And why not? Give somebody else a crack at it. However, there has never been since a feature quite like our *Doctor Who?* This is a boast I can expect, with confidence, to go completely and utterly unchallenged.

Bloody Ages Ago.

CHAPTER 18

The Very Last Straw

My cartooning collaborations with Mr Quinn had apparently now ceased, so he and I both went our merry ways. I was still obtaining cartooning commissions. I produced a small range of greetings cards, even seaside postcards. Another was for a delightful series of 'humour' books produced by Brockhampton Press, entitled *The Funny Book Of...* They were handy, 60-page pocket-sized, inexpensive publications, the sort you see on souvenir stall spinner racks. I contributed colour cartoons for the books, interspersed between the text 'jokes' which were selected by Karen Sullivan and Bob Hale. I was given very much a free hand and submitted roughs for selection. My cartoon subjects were 'Golf', 'Mothers In Law', 'Fathers' and 'After Dinner Stories'. I managed to infiltrate a *Doctor Who* gag with an 'after dinner speaker' Dalek giving a 'Knock Knock, Who's There' speech. Oh the wit of it all.

Back at Fleet Street, Gerald Lip, cartoon editor of the *Daily Star* ('*Star Fun*') was still buying my 'spot' cartoons. (*The Sun* and the *Daily Mirror* were now about the only other national press with a cartoon page. The *Mirror* also ran a short-lived feature cartoon series, to which I contributed, called *Funny Money*. No reflection on the fee, naturally).

Gerald Lip was a very nice guy and also a cartoonist himself and an excellent artist. However, Gerald got himself into a spot of bother. During the mid-1990s a newspaper 'war' erupted. A new London evening paper was produced and rival publishers attempted a 'spoiler'. They revived the old long-defunct *London Evening News* which was full of not much except quite a lot of my 'spot' cartoons. Gerald had asked me for anything 'London' themed, so I quickly submitted a batch of cartoons, most of which were printed in a single edition. Thus on one glorious *day* I earned £250! This enraged other cartoonists who incorrectly assumed that I had the sole rights to submit material . This eventually sorted itself and quite soon the 'new' old spoiler *London Evening News* vanished along with my nice little daily earner.

Early in 1997, Letts Educational publications contacted me. Would I please illustrate a series of 'primers'? Of course. The fee was an astounding £3,000. I began work at once producing full colour roughs of an apposite and humorous nature. Previously, I'd illustrated the *Which Guide To Hi Fi* and so I ploughed on in a similar vein in my usual inimitable way. Big shock. My commission was cancelled suddenly. Apparently the editorial team had decided, belatedly, on a single 'cute' character (a Smurf lookalike) with no 'humour' attached. This was being drawn by a piss poor in-house artist. So all that creative work down the drain. Thanks a lot! I eventually settled for 50% of the fee, but that was not the point. I had really looked forward to this commission and now it had been scuppered by some berk of an editor. So there and then I gave it all up. It was the year 1997 and I resolved never again to draw a cartoon for a paying publication.

CHAPTER 19

A Life in Television

My perambulations within the world of magazine feature scribing lead me inexorably to The British Amateur Television Club which as the name suggests is a club for British amateur television clubbers. Historically, it was during 1949 that the BATC (as abbreviated) was formed in order to promote 'Ham Television'. This was where electronics enthusiasts built their own licenced 'shack' TV stations (usually literally in a shack) and viewed each other (*hello G8 XYZ*) on restricted transmission bandwidths (usually 70cms). One impediment was that nothing smacking of 'entertainment value' was allowed to be broadcast. Witnessing recently these 'ham' transmissions, the TV clubbers are certainly still adhering to *that* golden rule.

I obtained a commission from a magazine called *Production Solutions* to cover the annual BATC Rally which was a vast boot fair and exhibition, an outing for members and families. In 1998 it was held at the Sports ConneXtion, near Coventry. I interviewed various people and took a few snaps for editorial use. Mostly, the conventioneers were intent of selling redundant equipment but others were on the hunt for memorabilia. One interviewee was John van Dyke a freelance floor manager – ex-BBC – who was look-

ing for anything connected with *The Black and White Minstrel Show*, books or tapes (the BBC have hardly any recordings of this programme). John had been floor manager for some of the early Minstrel colour recordings at BBC Television Centre and indeed married one of the dancers, so he had a specific interest.

Another interested party was Andy Emmerson. As mentioned earlier, Andy edited a nostalgia-driven, pre-colour TV magazine called *405-Alive*. I reported Andy as saying, 'These days it's only at electronics rallies like this that you can find old PYE monitors or perhaps back copies of ITV Yearbooks. That sort of nostalgia is getting hard to find and dealers are charging prices to match'. Indeed, current prices on eBay for 1960s copies of those ITV Yearbooks can now exceed £100.

Also, at one of these BATC Rallies, I had met electronics engineer Paul Marshall and by doing so, this chance meeting opened up an entirely new career for me, of which more later.

CHAPTER 20

Trust in TV

By now, I was a perceived as a 'Television History Expert'. Be that as it may, I had a least worked in the medium and had now begun to collect items of historic TV studio technical equipment. With these recommendations draped about me, I was invited to become, and as far as I can tell, still am, a member of an outfit called The Alexandra Palace Television Trust (not to be confused with the Alexandra Palace Trust or The Alexandra Palace Television Society).

The Television Trust's sole aim was to preserve for posterity the fabric of the two areas within Alexandra Palace which formed the original 1936 BBC television studios. This television trust was an adjunct to the main AP Trust. Both trusts functioned under the auspices of Haringey Council. It didn't help that both trusts were constantly besieged by a gaggle of self-interested 'developers', obstructionists and monumental egotists. Also, it didn't further the Television Trust's *raison d'etre* when a few of its own trustees were constantly at logger heads with each other and everybody else for that matter.

We bumbled along with tiresome monthly meetings, held sometimes at Alexandra Palace itself, but usually we had to meet a few miles away at an old converted former public convenience inhab-

ited currently then by the Hornsey Historical Society. One of my first suggestions as a Trustee, (and which was acted upon), was to shift all the 'exhibition' equipment (of which there was a motley and dilapidated collection) from the ground floor up to one of the studios. This made sense to me as it was a better venue to attract possible funds for our projected conducted tours. The studios themselves were in a neglected state. There were multiple holes in the roof, attendant scuttling vermin, pigeon poo and rickety flooring, the usual result of British indifference to its heritage.

It was in 1935 that the BBC chose a crumbling Victorian edifice in North London named Alexandra Palace to house its proposed new-fangled television service. Alexandra Palace was, at that time, a commercial white elephant containing several dilapidated exhibition areas, a theatre and a couple of interconnecting banqueting halls. These two halls, each thirty foot by seventy foot, were transformed into prototype television studios with electronic control areas, fitted adjacent. On one of the four corners of the building, a transmitter tower, still there, was positioned. This took advantage of the three hundred foot location height of Alexandra Palace which was ideal for the VHF transmitter beam. This had a 'line of sight' range of approximately thirty miles. In 1936, this was sufficient to cover a quarter of the population of the UK.

In mid-1936 BBC Television began operations but it soon became apparent that the Alexandra Palace studios were cramped and inconvenient. Added to which, the studios were situated on the first floor and so all the scenery, props and electronics had to be winched from ground level. Nevertheless, television prospered, and apart from a break during the second world war, the Alexandra Palace studios produced several memorable live programmes, not least of which was, in 1953, *The Quatermass Experiment*.

The Television Trust and I struggled on grimly, amidst petty shenanigans and needless point scoring. One of the aims of this Trust, or so I imagined, was to preserve and perhaps reinstate the old studios as an educational resource. To this end, an ill-conceived feasibility study, paid for by an Arts Council grant, was commissioned from a company of surveyors. Their eventual conclusion, after much delay, proved that creating an exhibition and projected

Alexandra Palace Studios in 1997.

four-wall studio hire area within the existing space was unfeasible. As somebody who had worked in TV, I was a little nonplussed that the survey company hadn't asked me one single question or even asked for advice. Many other fanciful schemes for the studios came and went, including demolition entirely. Latterly the studios, or at least one of them, was spruced up and currently is used by the BBC to impress visiting parties or to indoctrinate new staff members.

With Paul Marshall in 1997.

In 1996, the shambolic Television Trust just about managed to organise a 60th birthday party for the TV Studios and we invited several notables including the former BBC announcer, Sylvia Peters, who cut the celebratory cake and spoke a few well-chosen words. After, she allowed me to kiss her cheek which was very much a plus of the evening. All progressed reasonably smoothly, but I learned subsequently of an undercurrent of much ill-temper and bitchiness from certain Trust members. After much hand wringing and teeth sucking, I decided I'd had enough and called it a day. Trust me, I'm a Television Trustee. No thanks.

Later in 2011, a smaller scale celebration, this time the 75th anniversary was held, again, in Studio A. For this, the Bradford-based National Media Museum kindly loaned, from their collection, one of the original BBC Emitron studio cameras. Only a very few of this camera type were ever manufactured and only a handful, in various states of integrity, remain. I'm constantly surprised how *small* the Emitron camera was, until I remembered that most of the camera's control apparatus (the size of a large bedroom wardrobe) was tucked away in the bowels of Camera Control. The Museum's camera looked brand new, evidence that it had been well looked after (or perhaps extensively restored, because it certainly didn't look as if it had been subjected to the usual BBC TLC). During the party, and feeling a bit reckless, I managed to prise off the camera's top. Unfortunately, the Emitron's Iconoscope imaging tube was missing. Apparently, it was too fragile to risk installing for the exhibition. Understandable, when one considers that these tubes are quite rare and irreplaceable.

The Emitron camera.

Previously, I mentioned that my meeting with engineer Paul Marshall had proved fortuitous. Paul, an ex-Marconi employee, collected old, redundant and heavyweight television cameras, especially ones manufactured by the Marconi company. It was a crazy hobby as Paul would be the first to admit. All this early TV technology was, and is, weighty and space consuming. However, Paul had a particular interest which involved restoration and preservation coupled with his acknowledged talent for electronic knowhow.

Earlier, Paul had stored all his cameras and electronic bric-a-brac in his bachelor accommodation which was part of a three storey town-house in Sunrise Avenue, Chelmsford. This intrigued me because I too had lived in a three storey town house in Sunrise Avenue, Chelmsford. In fact Paul had lived in the *very same house*. It transpired that Paul had sub-let from a colleague, another Marconi engineer, who had bought the house from us when, in 1979, we had moved to a larger property a few miles away.

My conversation with Paul occurred at a BATC rally where Paul was exhibiting a few of his classic Marconi TV cameras. Naturally, I wanted some of *those!* I began at once to hunt for redundant TV camera equipment, a search which lead me to a local Chelmsford scrap heap and thence to an entirely new career, a career later involving me in award-winning television drama, Hollywood blockbuster movies and several exhibitions in the Royal palaces of England.

CHAPTER 21

Down Amongst the Junk

Reeling back to 1956 and that ATV Southend-on-Sea outside broadcast, with my younger self posing beside a real live TV camera, forty years later, I aimed to buy such a camera. Not easy, in fact, seemingly impossible. Most broadcast television camera equipment was manufactured in relatively small quantities and had a finite life span of ten years or so. After that period, TV companies scrapped or recycled the stuff. The BBC had its own redundant equipment store at Avenue House, Power Road, Chiswick. Sometimes the lucky recipients of these time-expired cameras were foreign 'emerging' broadcasters, or possibly educational establishments with nascent media courses. Once, I tracked down a likely camera but it was reposing, inconveniently, in a shed in Ethiopia!

My first old TV purchase was a pair of 1960s camera headphones. It was a start. But I was determined to acquire the big stuff and between 1992 and 1995 I took possession of a succession of classic electronic items including an EMI 2001 colour camera (ex-Anglia TV) a Pye Mk 3 (ex-ATV – yes, the very same type as depicted in my Southend photo!) an EMI 203 camera from Lime Grove Studios and a mighty 1950s era Marconi Mk III camera from the BBC Manchester Dickenson Road studios. These Man-

chester studios had previously produced the delights of such as *Top Of The Pops*, *Val Doonican* and *Pinky and Perky* so I can claim with confidence that my camera had truly rubbed shoulders with the musical elite. But it was now 1996 and I decided that it was time to build an extension to my home.

During the 1990s I was steadily building my collection which now included ancillary items such as microphones, studio lighting, lenses and tripods. Even a few movie cameras. I'm asked usually, how I find this equipment. Basically it's word of mouth or recommendation. An early lead was from an acquaintance who mentioned perhaps a camera or two might be buried under a pile of scrap at a Chelmsford metal reclaimers. This info didn't seem at all likely. However, on the off chance that this tip might prove correct, I visited the scrap yard and uncovered no less than *eight* ancient television cameras, all jumbled up and in various states of disrepair. These cameras, which dated from 1951, included two American models that had somehow drifted over from a Los Angeles TV station called KHJ-TV. Unbelievable.

Scrapyard camera heap.

It hadn't really occurred to me that my collection of television camera equipment could be used as props for movies or TV. But eventually this is precisely what happened. Those scrap cameras recovered from the Chelmsford junk yard, (and others), have since travelled the length of Europe appearing as authentic props in several movies, including a Dublin location (*Evelyn*) with Pierce Brosnan and another in Berlin (*Beyond The Sea*) with Kevin Spacey. Also, many home grown TV dramas including *The Hour* and the *Doctor Who* anniversary drama *An Adventure in Space and Time* (more of which later). Crowning this, in 2013 a special 60th Coronation Anniversary exhibition was held during the Summer months at Buckingham Palace, and yes, yet again one of those scrap yard cameras was on display, looking every bit the pristine original 1953 Marconi machine. Even, would you believe, in June of 2013 as a BBC Camera exhibit in the foyer for the opening ceremony of the Corporation's billion quid 'New' Broadcasting House. And so it goes.

Previously, Paul Marshall and I had agreed to split the hiring of our TV equipment. This meant that our by now substantial collections constituted an enormous catalogue, rivalling anything available anywhere in the world. To date, this arrangement has worked well. We call ourselves *Golden Age Television Recreations*, it's all in the name, but still we get enquiries from untutored tyro production assistants seeking spiral staircases, old chimney pots or hurricane lamps.

Silly requests aside, for the past twenty three years, Paul and I have provided a unique service, hiring items as small as a microphone up to a large outside broadcast truck. In 2005, we hit the big time when we shipped to Hungary, almost *four and a half tons* of vintage television and film equipment for a Universal Pictures movie project. Initially, this project was shrouded in secrecy with even sniffer dogs on set. Later it was revealed as being the Oscar nominated film *Munich*, the director, Steven Spielberg.

But why four and a half tons of movie props? It goes like this. Something called 'Show and Tell'. Mr Spielberg, as he was addressed, required a choice. We assembled and arranged all our shipped kit in an airfield hanger at one of the locations, and Mr

Spielberg came in, saw the 'show' and told us what he wanted. Expensive when considering that only about a third of our equipment was chosen and even less was seen in the final cut. Nevertheless, it was very much a master class in megabucks Hollywood blockbusting.

For *Munich* we spent a happy September week in Budapest, but as most of our scenes were scripted for shooting at night, we slept during the day and awoke to have our breakfast at 5.30 in the afternoon. Unsettling. Some major scenes took place at an old Soviet-era airfield called Tokol. During one night of shooting, I supervised the handling our props and when I returned early in the morning to the Budapest hotel, my wife counted ninety mosquito bites on my back. Strangely, during the shoot, I was totally unaware of the little nippers.

I had decided now to concentrate exclusively on camera-collecting and prop-hiring. Having already abandoned my cartooning career, I now gradually abandoned media writing. To be honest, I had just about covered everything and markets were changing yet again.

In 2006, Kelly Publications printed my book, *Television Innovations: 50 Technological Developments*, which was a compendium of some of my many media articles, illustrated with photographs. It was a nice little production and the cover price was not too expensive, (now available as a Kindle version). The book was intended as essentially, a non-technical media primer, produced to familiarise students with the history of television broadcast hardware and also for geeks who just liked drooling over images of old TV cameras. Whatever, sales were modest.

An early dip (February 1996) into the wonderful world of prop hire was via Keith Barnfather of Reeltime Pictures. Keith wanted me to supply two classic television cameras for one of his *Doctor Who* sell-through VHS tapes. This edition was called *I Was A Doctor Who Monster* and featured interviews with the poor sods who were routinely stuffed into a Dalek chassis or coated with colourful gunk in the name of TV terror. On this occasion, I co-opted my brother Stephen and between us we trundled the cameras, mics and pedestals to the former BBC Riverside Studios, near Ham-

mersmith. We prepared several scenes recreating past *Doctor Who* episodes using lookalike actors and a sink plunger representing a Dalek. Ex-Doc Sylvester McCoy presided with Sophie Aldred in attendance. All went reasonably sweetly and we met some nice people including actor Peter Hawkins, whom I remember primarily as the voice of Mr Turnip and Porterhouse the Parrot.

My ever-expanding camera collection required yet another move, this time into the rural Essex countryside. I needed a house with grounds in order to spread. My 'hobby' was going places and so was I. We found a detached house in a modest village, and promptly demolished the old wooden garage, erecting in its place a thirty-five foot 'play room', at least that's what I called it on the planning application.

We're Doomed! – The Making of Dad's Army
with the superb John Sessions as Arthur Lowe.

As a rule, wherever possible, I travel with my cameras to the various studios or locations. I do this to protect my precious things from careless handling. During shoots I assist and also I can usually inveigle the production into hiring me as an S.A. or Supporting Artist, even my wife Margaret achieved this during some studio

scenes for a BBC 2 drama *Making Of Dad's Army*. They dressed her fetchingly as 'Script Lady'. For all this, additional fees are paid and also a possible and fleeting appearance in the finished product. To date I've been a pretend cameraman in over sixty productions, spanning the decades, from the 1940s to the 1990s. However, the casual viewer will note that I never seem to age. Only my hair style alters from long to short and back again plus wearing the same old deathless combination of brown tie, brown trousers and brown woolly jumper.

Thus, fully browned off, Golden Age Television has helped recreate scenes from many iconic television programmes including *Steptoe and Son*, *Coronation Street*, The 1953 Coronation BBC broadcast (three times), *Sunday Night At The London Palladium*, *What's My Line*, *The Brains Trust*, *Double Your Money*, *Thunderbirds*, *This Is Your Life*, *Top Of The Pops*, *Pot Black*, *The Sky At Night*, *Dad's Army* and *Doctor Who*. Also television and film dramas recalling the lives of, in no particular order, Tommy Cooper, Cilla Black, Hughie Green, Tony Hancock, Fanny Cradock, Lord Lucan, Lord Longford, Bobby Darin, Diana Princess of Wales, Margaret Thatcher, Hattie Jacques, Paul Raymond, Morecambe and Wise, Elizabeth Taylor, Richard Burton, Richard Nixon, John Lennon, Laurel and Hardy, Mary Whitehouse, Brian Clough, George Best, Enid Blyton, Hurricane Higgins, Peter Sellers, Kenny Everett, Franklin D Roosevelt, Boy George, Eddie The Eagle, Paddington Bear and Sooty.

CHAPTER 22

Now is the Hour

In 2009, I was hired, along with one of my old 35mm movie cameras, to recreate a scene with actress Helena Bonham Carter who was playing the part of Enid Blyton for a BBC 4 drama called appropriately enough, *Enid*. I arrived at Longcross Studios (a former MOD tank factory and military test site near Chertsey) and installed my 1940s Wall newsreel camera for a Blyton family scene. For this we used a dressed lounge, one of the many rooms situated in a real mansion positioned in the grounds of the studios. I was then bundled over to costume and fitted with a period tweed (brown) suit and a moustache, ready to play my part as a 1943 'Pathe' newsreel cameraman.

The scene was set, with the Blyton family playing a game of Snakes and Ladders. On 'Action!' the real movie camera focussed on myself pretending to film Helena and the two child actors, all positioned in front of a roaring fire. As is the usual practice in films, the 'fire' is a combination of imitation fire-proof logs and a self-lighting gas burner that can easily be switched on and off between takes. At the final take the gas fire was extinguished. This held a fascination for one of the child actors who announced, 'That fire is fake!' to which Helena replied, 'We're *all* fake here, darling.'

My life of churning out cartoons for the penny dreadfuls was now well and truly over as my progress as prop supplier to the world became established. I recall also that the Winter of 2010/2011 was *very* cold. This was the period in which we filmed *The Hour*, a sorely underrated BBC 2 serial drama set in the world of BBC Television circa 1956. My task was to fully equip a Lime Grove television studio with correct period cameras, lights, microphones and picture monitors. Earlier, the production designer for the series, Eve Stewart, had visited my house for a chat. Eve (*Les Miserables, The King's Speech, The Damned United, Vera Drake*) was tasked with visualising, not only the studio spaces, but also the production offices and cutting rooms. Eve needed advice and also some idea of the 1950s television technology used. I gave Eve a conducted tour of my collection, pointing out relevant items such as cameras, pedestals, microphone booms, lamps, and also the practicalities of 'pretending' to make fifty year-old equipment work. I explained to Eve that the trick is to implant modern electronics and imperceptibly hide it within the original shell or casing. It's understood that, with generally tight budgets, TV productions can't afford to hang about if the old stuff packs up at the critical moment. A modern implant will run all day. Fit and forget. Smoke and Mirrors.

Golden Age TV was commissioned to supply all the TV studio and film equipment for both series of *The Hour*. The series was made by the estimable production company, Kudos. Paul and I had never before undertaken such an extended commission, but we rose to the occasion, installing three iconic Marconi television cameras, one perched on a mobile mechanical crane. I even wangled myself a small position as Script Consultant, checking for technical anachronisms and inconsistencies. Also, Paul and I resumed our on-screen roles as 'studio cameramen', wearing the same old dun coloured outfits! Incidentally, *The Hour* is (to date) the only BBC Television programme to give Golden Age TV an on-screen credit. Apparently humble props companies *never* get a BBC puff.

Eve Stewart's, eventual studio designs bore little resemblance to the 'real' Lime Grove, but that wasn't the point. The reconstructions had the feel of an old 1950s television studio, as well as be-

ing ergonomically built so that the Director of Photography could easily manoeuvre his high-definition, digital Arri Alexa camera, as and when required. *The Hour* starred Romola Garai, Dominic West, Ben Whishaw and the charming Anna Chancellor, who for some obscure reason, wanted to have her photograph taken with me. Must have been the heady attraction of my exotic brown woolly jumper!

The Hour *with Anna Cancellor.*

Ben Whishaw on the set of The Hour.

And was it cold in November 2010? You bet, especially at Hornsey Town Hall. The old Town Hall, near Crouch End in London, was built in the early 1930s. In 1986 it had been closed as redundant due to local authority mergers and changes. Since then the Town Hall had limped along as an arts centre and latterly as rental space for TV and movie productions. Some of the interior spaces of Hornsey Town Hall were used for the office and studio sequences of *The Hour*. The main large theatre space was reconstructed as Lime Grove Studio E. Adjoining offices were dressed as newsrooms, edits suites, even a night club for Series Two. Unfortunately, for us, the main theatre space was completely unheated and so we shivered most of the time despite several industrial space heaters blasting away during takes. The glamour of movie-making, you see?

Apart from making a few quid hiring my collection, a corollary is that I never know what will turn up next. Sometimes it's the same old pop video hire, using myself and one of my 'analogue' tube colour cameras to film the 'look' of a 1970s *Top of the Pops* recording. Every aspiring promo director thinks he or she has thought of that 'neat idea' first. Two dozen noisy shoots later, this is patently not the case.

What came completely out of the blue was a commission from the famous London store, Selfridges. They wanted Golden Age TV to dress *all* of their eleven Oxford Street windows with movie and video equipment. We were to supply cameras, tripods and lights. Our equipment was to complement various fashions provided by designers such as Stella McCartney, Paul Smith, Thom Brown, Yohji Yamamoto and Jean Paul Gaultier. Themed as 'The Masters', our cameras were positioned amongst the frocks and suits with oblique references to famous movies and directors. Not entirely successful perhaps, being a little esoteric, unless you were a film buff or a fan of expensive couture. Or both.

For these window dressings, our equipment had been shipped earlier to the Oxford Street store. Later, Paul and I assisted in assembling all the eleven windows. This had to be undertaken from 10pm when the store closed for the night. We were still there at 2am the following morning. Quite an experience, especially when

three months later we repeated the process and repacked everything, again well into the wee small hours. Thus the Summer of 2014 was a proverbial showcase for our cameras. Coincidentally, I'd also tailored another window display (an Auricon 16mm movie camera) which featured in the Old Bond Street upmarket clothing store DAKS. All told, 2014 was quite a shop window for Golden Age Television.

Selfridges window.

During 2015, I was involved in a variety of productions that included *Father Brown*, *Call the Midwife* and *Making of Dad's Army*, filmed in and around the interesting city of Belfast. Also a five-part TV drama series entitled *SS-GB* based on the 'what if the Nazis had won the war' novel by Len Deighton. Filming of one sequence, a joint Nazi/Soviet ceremony, took place at Highgate Cemetery. The Call Sheet for the day advised all to 'be aware of the sensitive nature of the programme and the possible upset that could be caused to the general public. Ensure that no costume or insignia are visible to the general public when leaving the set...' in other words, no goose stepping around Golders Green in the lunch break, thank you very much!

Ely, August 2015. Recreating the 1953 coronation broadcast.

Ely, August 2015. Golden Age movie camera prop.

Golden Age Television also filmed at Ely Cathedral. We provided camera props for part of a mammoth, hundred million quid drama series produced by Netflix entitled *The Crown*, this was a very much expanded version of Peter Morgan's theatre production *The Audience*. This sixty part production – yes, sixty parts! – follows the life and times of Her Majesty, with Matt Smith no less as the Duke of Edinburgh! We helped recreate not only the BBC television 1953 coronation broadcast but also the newsreel sequence of Princess Elizabeth's wedding in 1947. Ely Cathedral stood in, on both occasions, for Westminster Abbey. This might seem a bit perverse. So why not use the real building? But general practicalities always preclude this, especially in the heart of London. Usually, if a central London location is needed, the best time to film is early Sunday morning. But Ely Cathedral was fine and looked the part, even if the frigid wind whipping around the cloisters appeared to come direct from the Urals.

Another interesting experience was working on a big Hollywood movie, *The Infiltrator*, starring *Breaking Bad* actor Bryan Cranston. *The Infiltrator* purports to be a dramatic recreation of money laundering, drugs and the 1980s BCCI financial scandal. Our scenes, posing as NBCTV News cameramen, this time wearing dinner jackets, were set during an elaborate wedding reception in a Florida ballroom circa July 1988. But in reality, filmed at a chilly hotel complex in Copthorne, West Sussex in March 2015. Ah, the magic of the movies. We shiver and shake for our art.

My part in *The Infiltrator* required me to actually film for real. I had supplied a 1980s vintage Sony Betacam BVP3 (anorak info) video camera and I was required to record a wedding sequence, the taped images to be intercut later within the main footage. During a scene the FBI suddenly appear and break up the proceedings, charging in with guns and dogs. Lots of noise and racing about. Very dynamic. They hadn't told me that I was going to be physically restrained from filming, and I got a hefty whack from a charging extra, which bruised my eye and dislodged my finger from the camera's record button. The director loved it.

Now, these early professional camcorders were not exactly

Bewigged Infiltrator.

lightweight objects. As my task was to wander around the set with one balanced on my shoulder the weight of this camera, and the long hours standing about, prompted me to pad my shoulder (under my jacket) with a quantity of bubble wrap. Unfortunately, every time I hoisted the camera onto my shoulder, ready to shoot, a loud 'popping' resulted, sounding like muffled gun shots. Bryan Cranston, awaiting his cue, remarked that my joints must be wearing out. I earned my money that day.

Part of Dicky's extensive vintage TV camera collection.

CHAPTER 23

An Adventure

It's now time to jump back some biographical years. It's 2013 and the 50th anniversary of the *Doctor Who* programme. BBC2 had commissioned a celebratory drama and the producers sensibly came to the only guys on the planet capable of (again) recreating Lime Grove Studios, namely, Paul and me. This time the old BBC LG studio D (demolished in 1991) was erected at the salubrious Wimbledon Studios, and for two weeks we all wallowed in TV nostalgia. Ace writer Mark Gatiss had lovingly crafted a script that beautifully recaptured the genesis of the programme. The story featured an eerily exact recreation of the original pilot episode studio recording. Noted character actor David Bradley played with exactitude William Hartnell playing Doctor Who. Other cast members included Claudia Grant as Susan, Jamie Glover as Chesterton and Jemma Powell as a spot-on Barbara. Paul and I installed our cameras, lights and gallery monitors and yes, yet again, undertook our old timeless roles as television cameramen, wearing itchy beige pullovers and oily minimalist haircuts.

An Adventure in Space and Time began filming in February of 2013 with the 1963-era Lime Grove studio recreations taking about two weeks to complete. Our cameras again, were 'pretend

live', in fact the same equipment as used on *The Hour*. Picky purists may have said that our cameras were not the exact models used in Studio D on the first *Doctor Who* programmes. We countered that our cameras were certainly used next door in Studio E, and in any case, none of the original *Doctor Who* Studio D cameras now exist for prop hire purposes.

TARDIS.

Our three Marconi cameras all had viewfinders that functioned and the red lights that glowed nicely when switched on. The camera's images were fed from the studio floor, directly to the gallery monitors. It all looked pretty authentic. Those pesky picky purists could probably tell that our 'old format' black and white images were somewhat too clean and sharp to pass for the real 1963 thing. The BBC sell-through DVD of the programme maintained the fiction that our cameras images were real. Not so. However, nothing broke down, everything ran all day and importantly, on cue. A little later, the director Terry McDonough created a break down all on his own.

Terry is a lovely chap and a skilled director but he was not so good with his hands. During a scene change, Terry decided to

An Adventure... *cast.*

Mark Gatiss takes a family photo.

Recreating a scene in An Adventure in Space and Time.

Marco Polo reimagined.

assist the props department and attempted to move one of our vintage 1960s trolleys with a monitor perched on top. Unfortunately, at that moment one of the trollies wheels came off and our precious original period monitor crashed to the floor. Fortunately there was no damage, apart from a small dent. They built 'em tough in those days. Not so amusing was later, when I very nearly put actor Brian Cox, playing Sydney Newman, in hospital. I was manoeuvring one of our heavy pedestals in preparation for a sequence and in an absent moment, bumped Brian in the back of his knees and the poor chap teetered, alarmingly. Fortunately, Brian regained his balance as I sheepishly reversed the ped in the nick of space and time.

I mentioned earlier I had had the pleasure of speaking with Carole Ann Ford. Other well-known actors wandered into the studio from time to time including Tom Goodman-Hill, Mr Grove from ITV's popular drama series *Mr Selfridge*. I'd met Tom previously when he had played a fleeting role as David Frost in a movie, filmed during 2007 called *Hippy Hippy Shake*. This controversial film, starring amongst others, Cillian Murphy, Sienna Miller, Chris O'Dowd, Lee Ingelby and Hugh Bonneville, purported to depict the UK's 1970s 'alternative culture'. The plot revolved around the concurrent underground press with the trial of the notorious *OZ* magazine 'School Kids Issue' featuring prominently. Golden Age TV supplied various camera props including parking one of our large outside broadcast vehicles (Southern Television) on a private airfield in Buckinghamshire for a 'TV outside broadcast' scene. Our van was hired to help recreate the shambolic 1970 Isle of Wight pop festival. Sex, drugs and rock and roll? You bet! For this section of the movie, the airfield was bedecked with a large collection of prop 'merchandise' stalls, performance areas and lighting towers, plus an army of extras dressed as happy hippies. *Too* happy hippy as it turned out. Apart from the second camera unit filming a naked couple 'balling' (authentic 1970s term) behind our OB truck, what was most prevalent was the sweet smell of weed drifting all around. This was rather too much for the local Bucks constabulary, who arrived at reckless speed in true motorised *Sweeney* fashion to put a stop to all the fun. Sadly, despite the artistic effort and expense (north of £20 million), *Hippy Hippy Shake* sank with

all on board. This movie, which had one or two preview show-ings, was never released theatrically or dumped onto DVD. Finally, the unhappy hippy movie was shelved somewhere in a dark back room. If reports are given credence, the entire negative was then subsequently and irrevocably shredded.

Returning to the impressive set of *An Adventure in Space and Time*, the specially constructed Daleks used in the production were superb in every detail. I can attest to his having actually ridden in one of the originals. This occurred during the 1960s when I worked at Alexandra Palace, lending a hand with the annual BBC staff kids' Christmas party. As a timely surprise, we shipped from TV Centre your actual Dalek and I just had to have a ride, didn't I? My gosh, what an intractable object it was. All creaky wood and tatty bent tin. Not at all easy to shift, crouched inside, as one was, perched on a narrow bench, castors at each corner, trying to push along the bloody thing!

Acting at the console.

During a break in filming *An Adventure...* I spotted Peter Capaldi admiring the wonderfully recreated, and expensive, TARDIS control console. I introduced myself and reminded him

that we had worked together on Series Two of *The Hour*. He remembered our association and I asked Peter whether he was a *Doctor Who* fan. He averred that he held a mild interest. 'I quite like the programme, Dicky...' Later it was announced to all the world that he would be the next Doctor, so I suppose he really did 'quite like' the programme? The filming of *An Adventure in Space and Time* was a delight, a real highlight. As a lasting memento, I have a cast-signed shooting script. Oh yes!

And so onward, towards a continuing adventure in space and time, even to the extent of once again collaborating with Mr T Quinn and having published in 2015 a sell-out edition of our collected *Who* works, *It's Even Bigger on the Inside*.

Later, in an idle moment I mentioned to my patient wife Margaret that perhaps it would be nice to have an autobiography of my working life, as an inspiration or perhaps a dire warning? She retorted with familial logic, 'Who'd want to read that?' Well, I do for a start, my dear. And I hope you've enjoyed it. In fact, no time to dwell because recently Tim and I were commissioned to produce a new one-off *Doctor Who* cartoon strip for the 500th edition of the *Doctor Who Magazine*...

Now, where did I put that flippin' pen...?

1960.

Tate Gallery exhibition.

Bayford Lodge, 1 College Avenue, Epsom (21103)

Dicky Howett Esq
118 Sunrise Ave.,
Chelmsford
Essex

Dear Mr Howett.

Very many thanks for your letter. The
answer is yes, of course, but I'm afraid
you'll have to go on the end of a
waiting list!

As soon as I can I will

Regards

Frank Hampson

Letter from Frank Hampson.

Dicky at work. Serious business, humour.

Dicky's scrapbook.

Dicky's scrapbook.

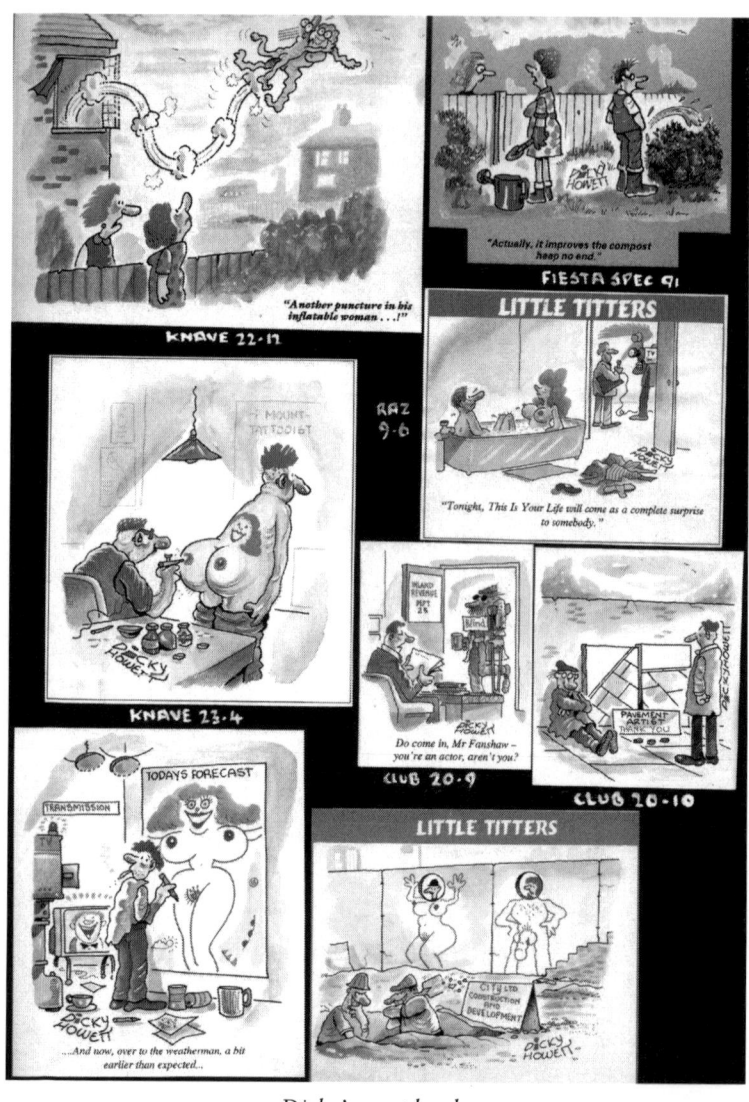

Dicky's scrapbook.

1986 Humour fest.

PUNCHLINES WORKSHOPS

FESTIVAL OF COMEDY 86 DER — ALL EVENTS FREE!

Bluecoat Gallery

During the last two weeks of PUNCHLINES there will be a series of afternoon workshops in the gallery given by some of the cartoonists featured in the exhibition, as part of the Festival of Comedy programme. All these events are FREE and open to any age group.

TIM QUINN + DICKY HOWETT
Weds 16th July at 2.00p.m.

Quinn and Howett have gained a national reputation through their work for D. C. Thompson's 'Celebrity' magazine, Target Books and their 'Dr. Who' comic strips. Both artists will be continuing a comic strip in the gallery and will be available to answer questions and discuss their work.

ERIC JONES
Thurs 17th July at 2.00p.m.

Featured in the local section of Punchlines, Eric Jones is a graphic artist currently working at the Crawford Art Centre. During the afternoon he will be inviting people to contribute to a comic-strip story to be completed by the end of the event.

POSY SIMMONDS
Weds 23rd July at 2.00p.m.

With her regular Silent Three comic strip in The Guardian, Posy Simmonds has achieved a reputation as one of the most astute and humorous observers of middle class trendiness. Posy will be at the gallery to sign copies of her books and to talk about her work.

God! Some people are still trying to force their children into rigid MALE/FEMALE stereotypes.

BILL TIDY
Thurs 24th July 2.30p.m.

Bill Tidy whose work was recently exhibited in a major show at the Walker Art Gallery makes a welcome return to Merseyside, to talk about the joys of living in Walsall! During the afternoon Bill will be demonstrating how he draws his cartoons, and he may even draw a few members of the audience. Children particularly welcome.

POSDYKES TRIPE
THE FOOD OF
THE 90DS!

Further details of all events, please contact Bryan Biggs at Bluecoat Gallery, School Lane, Liverpool L1 3BX. Tel: 051 - 709 5689.

Supported by Merseyside Arts.

BACK
TRACKS

Dicky Howett considers the merits of CD sound and goes in search of the ideal theme music

It takes a bit of getting used to. CD sound I mean. Mind you, it's certainly miles better than woolly old vinyl. I must confess that the sound of compact discs came as a surprise.

For years, my ears have been tuned to snaps, crackles and pops and that familiar 'hush' and rumble as the old LP grinds up to speed. Nowadays, my gleaming new Philips 624 CD player bangs in without a word of warning or a hint of mechanism and off it goes, cleanly sweeping all before it.

Slot in a favourite classic (pop or Puccini) and every little twang, plink and plonk is faithfully reproduced, along with various orchestral creaks and squeaks and paper-like rustles.

It's all there. Bassoonists breathing. Piccolo players puckering lips. At least that's what it *sounds* like. Very atmospheric.

But compact disc technology can be utterly merciless with analogue transfers. All the recording faults are brutally exposed. Some AAD or ADD reissues burst out like sizzling sausages. Dog-eared old analogue master tapes can be heard to flutter as they spool off at the end of a tune.

Of course, careful re-mastering can alleviate the worst of these imperfections. Although, as one recording engineer pointed out to me recently, too much digital jiggery-pokery can rip out the 'heart' of analogue performances, rendering the end result as something fit only for a Cyberman's ears.

Technophiles might cringe, but if the original recording steams and hisses like a leaky kettle, then leave it be. That's how it is, man.

My very own contribution to the art of radio (and I use the word 'art' advisedly) is a recorded series of sardonic short stories entitled *Tall Tales Of Essex*.

These items have been featured (despite the occasional listener complaint) since 1986 on one of the larger BBC local radio stations, BBC Essex.

Each 'tale' recalls a pseudo-historical event in Essex, is backed by music and canters along merrily for some five minutes. The final taped mix is the usual BBC studio-quality production (15 ips stereo). It's all done in a frightful rush, local radio studio time being at a premium.

Apart from the negligible task of actually thinking up the stories, my main headache each recording session is finding suitable music to match the theme of the Tale.

The music mustn't be too raucous and no vocals thank you. This can be limiting.

My own disc collection (about 150 LPs plus CDs and jumble sale rejects) reflects my eclectic approach to tunes, but collapses when confronted with the occasional requirement for early Southend bongos or late Clacton castanets.

BBC Essex has its own record library to meet the immediate needs of the station — MOR, classic hits, no hard rock. The library has, neatly stored in dedicated racks, 6,000 discs and 16,000 catalogued tracks.

This might seem a lot, but is nothing compared to its big brother BBC Gramophone Library in London, which boasts 1¼ million commercial discs and is expanding at the rate of 1000 new additions each month.

My hunt for musical miscellany inevitably leads me to Alison Hartley, who is the BBC Essex record librarian.

Alison can access most daily requirements from stock, but lately the programme selection and choice of music is made by a machine called SABLE.

This forms part of a computerised system (ILR stations use a different model) which spews out on a daily basis the 'records of the day' menu.

SABLE — studio automatic barcode logging equipment — enables programme presenters to eschew the tedious task of actually choosing tunes.

Alison will program in their choices, coupled with the station's desired music profile and the stringent limitations on local radio needle time (currently only three hours per day for BBC Essex).

SABLE then digests overnight, cogitates over a selection of some 3,000 tracks, mixes them all up, and produces for the following morning a (hopefully) coherent and non-repetitive running order.

Each listed musical item is identified by a reference number giving full details of when it was recorded, what position it held in the hit parade, the running time, and how long the intro is (important for gabby DJs).

When the ditty is played on-air the barcode on the running sheet is 'wiped' and all important details (financial) are logged for issue to the various performing rights organisations.

Exceptions to all this needle time logging are tracks from obscure Dutch imports or taped copies of music lifted directly off movie soundtracks.

The Performing Rights Society monitors all radio broadcasts on a rotating basis three days a month to ensure all monies are duly coughed up.

The BBC Essex record library has, to date, only a modest selection of CDs (compilations of old hits are favoured, or 'comp mixed' as they are referred to) and Alison is aiming at an eventual storage ratio of 70 per cent compact discs.

It would appear that the sheer robustness of the silver disc is proving a big hit, castanets and bongos not withstanding. ▲

Next issue: Dicky encounters a few audio problems.

In next month's Complete CD

Crunching the digits – We look at four top players all using different D-A conversion. How and why do they sound different?

Exploring the digital domain – An investigation into how CDs are made.

Killer B & O – Bang and Olufsen's carry-about CD system offers lifestyle design and the ultimate in electronic control. But is it worth the £2,000 asking price?

The collector's guide to psychedelia – Mind-blowing music returns to haunt us. But now it's available on CD. Ashley Norris reports.

DAT's Big Daddy – JVC's XD-Z1010 flagship DAT recorder on test.

Managing the midi muddle – Rick Maybury looks at trying and buying midi hi-fi.

June issue on sale May 9th. Complete CD And Hi-Fi Buyer. Spinning into the Nineties.

Complete CD *magazine.*

157

With Deborah Watling...

...Sophie Aldred...

159

...and Mr Quinn and Caroline Munro.

Dicky and the showgirl (plus camera).

Also Available:

Available literally now.

q

Also Available:

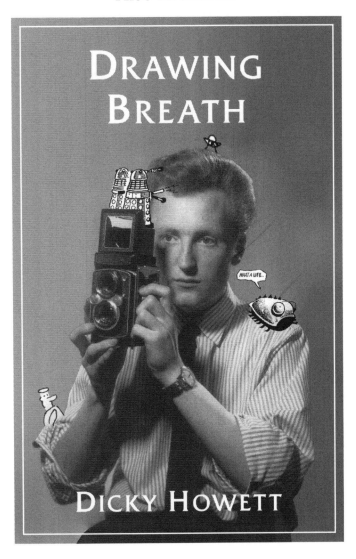

DRAWING
BREATH

WHAT A LIFE.

DICKY HOWETT

Available literally now.